MW01258710

About Island Press

Since 1984, the nonprofit organization Island Press has been stimulating, shaping, and communicating ideas that are essential for solving environmental problems worldwide. With more than 1,000 titles in print and some 30 new releases each year, we are the nation's leading publisher on environmental issues. We identify innovative thinkers and emerging trends in the environmental field. We work with world-renowned experts and authors to develop cross-disciplinary solutions to environmental challenges.

Island Press designs and executes educational campaigns, in conjunction with our authors, to communicate their critical messages in print, in person, and online using the latest technologies, innovative programs, and the media. Our goal is to reach targeted audiences—scientists, policy makers, environmental advocates, urban planners, the media, and concerned citizens—with information that can be used to create the framework for long-term ecological health and human well-being.

Island Press gratefully acknowledges major support from The Bobolink Foundation, Caldera Foundation, The Curtis and Edith Munson Foundation, The Forrest C. and Frances H. Lattner Foundation, The JPB Foundation, The Kresge Foundation, The Summit Charitable Foundation, Inc., and many other generous organizations and individuals.

The opinions expressed in this book are those of the author(s) and do not necessarily reflect the views of our supporters.

When Driving Is Not an Option

When Driving Is Not an Option

STEERING AWAY FROM CAR DEPENDENCY

Anna Letitia Zivarts

ISLANDPRESS | Washington | Covelo

Library of Congress Control Number: 2023948308

All Island Press books are printed on environmentally responsible materials.

Manufactured in the United States of America
10 9 8 7 6 5 4 3 2 1

Keywords: The Americans with Disabilities Act (ADA), automobile insurance, autonomous vehicle (AV), car dependency, choice nondrivers, delivery service, disability, disabled person, housing affordability, immigration status, involuntary nondrivers, micromobility, mobility, paratransit, parking reform, public transit, remote access, rideshare, sidewalk, transit access, walkability, wheelchair user

Contents

Foreword

Dani Simons, VP Public Affairs and
Communications for the Americas, Alstom

For the vast majority of my career, I have been trying to convince Americans to drive less. I have done this because it is a critical part of slowing and reversing the damage we have done to our planet. In theory, it should also help people improve their personal health and the health of their communities. It should make travel less expensive, helping people to keep more of their income for their families instead of putting it in the pockets of oil executives. I say "in theory" and "should" because these benefits are still largely theoretical in most of the United States. In order to achieve them we need to change the way we design our policies and our streets, the way we plan and price transit systems, our development incentives, and our zoning codes.

Before the pandemic three in four commuters in the US drove alone. The average length of a commute was thirteen miles, a distance not easily covered by walking or biking. According to

Governing magazine, taking transit for these trips took, on average, 1.5–1.9 times longer than driving alone.[1]

I have come to believe (despite much of what we see each day on social media) that most Americans are inherently rational—at least when it comes to their transportation decisions.

You cannot at any meaningful scale convince people to do things that go so far against their own self-interest, such as biking with their kids to school without safe infrastructure or waiting for a bus that only comes twice an hour in near-freezing temperatures on the side of the road with no bus shelter.

Yet as Anna's book points out, there are many in this country, nearly one-third of our population, who have no other options.

We are failing people who cannot and do not drive, diminishing their quality of life and hindering their social and economic opportunities. These failures hold back our local and regional economies. As a result, we're not able to make the strides necessary to fight the climate crisis, improve public health, and create a more just and equitable nation for all.

I was part of a team at the US Department of Transportation in the Biden-Harris administration that won the passage of a once-in-a-generation investment in American infrastructure. The bipartisan infrastructure law, or the Infrastructure Investment and Jobs Act (IIJA) as it is formally known, is an opportunity for us to change transportation. It, along with the COVID-19 funding that came before it, represents the largest investment that the US has ever made in transit or in passenger rail. It has a first-of-its kind program dedicated to improving roadway safety with $1 billion a year for five years.

My colleagues across USDOT also helped to craft policies meant to encourage states to use more of their highway funding to repair existing roads and in doing so create more "complete streets" and improve roadway safety instead of just expanding facilities.

The federal government has a vital role in making these kinds of transformations. But the projects that are funded are inherently local. That's a good thing, but it also means that all of us need to be vigilant, be engaged, and make ourselves heard as we work plan by plan, project by project, to change the way we do transportation. As Anna points out, we will only be able to truly transform transportation if we listen to the needs of people who do not have the option to drive.

We must shift from a worldview where the system is centered on people who drive to one that is centered on people who need to get somewhere and who deserve a variety of options. We need to shift to a worldview that meets our collective need for a planet where our children can breathe the air and live free from the increasingly frightening rumblings of climate change, for a nation where all residents can participate in society and the economy and where we're not spending extra hours a day waiting on a bus or walking and biking miles out of our way to keep ourselves safe.

Anna's book is a wake-up call and a roadmap to some of the policies and practices we should all be advocating for so this burden does not fall just on those who cannot drive but can be shouldered by all who want a more sustainable, healthy, and just nation.

Preface

It probably wasn't much past five o'clock, but it was dark and drizzling, as it does most of the winter in the Pacific Northwest, and so it might as well have been midnight. My friend Lara picked me up at my parents' house in the woods, driving an old faded, mint-green pickup truck that belonged to her mom. Both Lara and her mom were six feet tall, and because I was shorter, Lara always felt a little older to me, even though we were in the same grade. She spent a lot of time working on tall ships and prided herself on being just as strong as the guys. I envied her independence and wanted to be as tough and self-reliant as I imagined she was. So that night when she offered to teach me how to drive, even though I should have refused, I was pretty excited.

I was sixteen and I knew at that point I wasn't going to be able to get a driver's license. When all my friends were getting their permits, my parents took me to the DMV to see if I could pass the vision test. I remember standing at the counter, placing my head up to the chunky black vision testing apparatus. At the far end of the dark tunnel flickered a small yellow shape. Was it a letter? Was it a number? I couldn't tell. We left, me in tears.

I was born with a neurological condition called nystagmus that makes my eyes wiggle and bounce. When I'm awake, they're always wiggling and bouncing a little bit, and it becomes more pronounced when I'm tired or stressed. Researchers don't yet understand what causes nystagmus. Sometimes it's hereditary and linked to albinism, and so researchers have wondered if it's a response the brain develops to a weakness in the anatomy of the eye.

Some people get nystagmus later in life as a result of a brain injury. For them, it's much more disruptive. They perceive the world wiggling and shaking, as their eyes do, and that can result in migraines and dizziness. My brain, having had nystagmus since infancy, has figured out ways to cope. The world doesn't bounce around for me, but I don't see better than 20/80 on a vision chart. This means I can't see faces across a room or read text on a projector screen, blackboard, or a wall-mounted restaurant menu. When someone says hi to me, unless they're right next to me, I won't be able to recognize who they are, and trying to find people in a crowd is awful. But because when you look at me, you wouldn't at first guess that I have nystagmus, or even know what it is, acquaintances often think I'm just rude or ignoring them when I fail to wave back or say hello.

As a child born almost a decade before the Americans with Disabilities Act (ADA), I grew up with a deep sense of shame around my vision. And I felt intense pressure to camouflage my disability and to pretend I could see things I couldn't to keep others around me comfortable. I didn't know anyone else who was blind or low vision. Even in books or school, the only blind person I read about was Helen Keller, her long white petticoats firmly grounding her in another time that had little relation to me, on the sideline of a middle school PE game after getting smashed in the face, again, with a volleyball I didn't see in time to duck.

I wanted to be dateable, attractive, not the awkward kid I saw in photos with thick glasses, a head tilt, and eyes that couldn't find the camera. Like the ugly duckling or Cinderella, I figured if I worked hard enough at masking, nobody would know I was disabled, and my life would be immeasurably better. I stopped using the binoculars I needed to read the board at school. I always pretended I could see something when someone asked. And when Lara offered to teach me how to drive, I was all in, despite the fact it was dark, raining, and it was her mom's truck that we both knew I wasn't supposed to be driving.

Lara drove us to one of the empty parking lots at a nearby college campus. Each row of parking spaces was divided by a grassy median planted with trees. This campus, all modernist water-stained concrete, was built in the 1970s, so by the late 1990s, many of these trees had grown some heft.

We started out slowly and I was doing great. First gear, no problem, then second, third. By the time we were working on shifting into fourth gear, I had to get more speed. Suddenly, in one of the turns, there was a curb sticking out that I didn't see in time. We careened up over the curb, through the grass, and straight up the trunk of a thick fir tree.

Luckily, we were both uninjured, but the truck sustained considerable damage. I remember shaking from the cold and nerves as we tried to push the truck down off the tree, its hood crumpled.

I am incredibly thankful we weren't seriously hurt and didn't hurt someone else. And I'm also grateful that I had this experience, for while it took me another fifteen years to be comfortable enough to openly tell people about my disability, this crash gave my teenage self the knowledge that I could not safely drive.

Looking back now, I'm embarrassed that as a teenager, I didn't learn how to use the bus system in my town. Yes, it would have been a two-mile walk down rural roads to the nearest bus stop, but even that would have given me some sense of freedom. But I didn't know how to use the bus, and I definitely never met other adults who couldn't drive. I couldn't imagine a future for myself in Washington State where I would have the independence and ease of movement I craved, so I was intent on getting out.

I moved to the Bay Area for college, and New York City after that, where I'd heard there was a subway system, the only one in the country that never stopped running. Twenty-four-hour service represented freedom to me, equality with my peers back in the Pacific Northwest who could grab their keys and go whenever they wanted. But seventeen years later, after having a child, the desire to be closer to family back in Washington pulled my partner and me to move back.

As much as I appreciated being closer to family, the move away from a city where transit access had given me near-equivalent mobility with my nondisabled friends was difficult. In Seattle, I felt resentful every time I looked up directions on how to get somewhere on the bus and my phone showed it would take two to three times as long as it would if I could drive there. What would be a fifteen-minute drive would be an hour-and-a-half, multi-bus trip, where missing bus shelters meant me and my toddler would be waiting on the side of a loud arterial in the rain, covered in grit from the puddle splashes of passing Subarus.

But very quickly, I came to see I wasn't alone. Because of my job at a disability rights organization, for the first time in my life, I started meeting other disabled adults who couldn't drive. And

I started to hear stories about how missing sidewalks and curb cuts, broken transit station elevators and blocked crosswalks, infrequent buses, and a lack of affordable housing anywhere with decent transit service were making it hard for disabled people to be engaged in our communities, to work or go to school, and even to remain out of institutions like nursing homes. And I knew it wasn't only disabled people who didn't have reliable or affordable transportation. Having worked for many years with labor unions organizing low-wage, mostly immigrant service workers, I knew that transportation barriers impacted many people outside the disability community as well.

In Seattle, the route 7 bus that I took to and from work was always packed. I'd have to negotiate room for my toddler and his stroller to squeeze in with the other moms, many of them immigrants from East Africa, with seniors pushing grocery carts returning from shopping trips in the International District, with young men getting off at Lowe's to look for work as day laborers, with blind and deafblind workers on the way home from their shifts at the Lighthouse, with groups of high school students in the afternoons. Sitting on the 7, I started to think about what it would take to build a coalition with everyone on that bus, where we could fight for more reliable transit, for smoother sidewalks and nicer bus stops, for affordable housing close to where we needed to go.

In the fall of 2020, I had the opportunity to launch that vision with the creation of the Disability Mobility Initiative at Disability Rights Washington. My first goal was making nondrivers visible. I was tired of hearing from elected leaders that "everyone" in their communities drove, so spending more money on bus service or sidewalks just wasn't necessary. I knew it wasn't true, and I wanted to show that there were people—their constituents—on every street, in every community who couldn't drive. I set out to track down, interview, and document the stories of nondrivers from each of our state's legislative districts.

I figured it would be difficult. In a previous gig, I worked for the American Civil Liberties Union (ACLU) to identify plaintiffs who lacked state ID cards or birth certificates for challenges to voter identification laws. For one project, I'd gone to every soup kitchen in Wichita, Kansas, and asked everyone who would talk with me if they had ID and wanted to be able to vote; on another, I'd scrambled to find someone to drive me in the middle of a snowstorm to Wausau, Wisconsin, to track down a senior who showed me how her birth was recorded in the family Bible. She had never had a birth certificate and was worried with the new voter identification laws that she would not be able to vote.

Finding the people with these experiences took a lot more effort than posting on Facebook. While I knew it would be relatively easy to find car-free urbanists or influencer disability activists to share their stories, the people I most wanted to talk with were unlikely to be connected to the existing networks of transit, biking, or disability activism. But I knew that it was these stories, from people who usually remained invisible to policymakers, that would have the most profound impact on shifting the narrative that our transportation system, and car dependency more broadly, was working for us. And so, I knew it was worth the effort.

I started with the same approach I'd used working for the ACLU: reaching out to everyone I thought might have connections to nondrivers in their communities—not just transit agencies or nonprofits that provide rides to seniors and people with disabilities, but also groups that work with refugee communities, labor unions, and environmental justice organizers. Soon I had 75, then 100, then 250 stories from nondrivers. I heard stories not just from the big cities where buses run on Sundays, I also heard from people in small agricultural towns on the border with Idaho, up river valleys in the woods above old logging towns, from islands connected to the mainland by ferry, from all forty-nine of our state's legislative districts.[1]

And it wasn't just the stories that I gathered through the interviews—I was building relationships and creating an advocacy network. I was beginning to organize that coalition that I'd dreamed about while I was riding the 7 bus. So, when the time came to weigh in on transportation investments, people who previously had not had their voice considered were suddenly visible.

And more than just visible, most everyone I had the chance to interview was eager to be involved in advocating for changes that would improve our access. Unlike drivers who can grab the keys and quickly get somewhere, those of us without this privilege have spent hours and hours planning routes, coordinating drivers, waiting for buses, trying to find the most accessible and least unpleasant route to a grocery store. We've thought about the transportation system a lot. And as we're standing there, waiting for a gap in traffic and watching the bus that comes once every thirty minutes drive away before we could get to the stop, we've thought about what has to change to make things work better for us.

This expertise, from using the system day in and day out, is critically needed right now to lead us away from the damage that was caused, and that continues to be caused, by car dependency. It's not just the isolation, depression, and lack of community connections or access to critical services experienced by those of us who aren't able or can't afford to drive; it's also the disproportionate public health risks that communities that prioritize automobility place on poor, Black, Brown, and immigrant residents from air and noise pollution and the inevitable crashes, causing injury and death. Bigger than all that, there is the harm from the chaos of climate change that our reliance on automobility is locking in for our children and future generations.

From April through October my child wakes up every morning and checks the Air Quality Index before switching to the wild-fire layer on Google Maps to track where the smoke might be coming from. This is the world he will inhabit, a world where no place is protected from the smoke, the more frequent hurricanes, the stronger tornado-spawning thunder cells, or higher king tides. Where climate-induced displacement and migration from crop failure or unsurvivable heat waves will reshape our communities as we create space for climate refugees.

It is easy to feel defeated when considering the scale of the challenges. But we know that if we don't act to reduce emissions now, the disruption our children will have to survive will be even worse. And we know that our transportation system—in particular the way we have built our communities to work for, and mostly only work for, cars—is the largest contributor to emissions, and something that we have the power to change. We have to make it easier for everyone to get around more easily without driving. It's a moral imperative, not just for those of us who can't drive, but for the environmental health of our communities and the mitigation of climate change for our children.

I write this book from a place of hope. Not only because parenting gives me little choice, but because I have seen how much excitement and knowledge exists among those of us who can't drive, especially those of us who know that it will never be available for us, to fundamentally rethink society's car dependency. I know if we can put this passion into practice, change is not only possible, but inevitable.

Figure 0-1: Me and my kid waiting for the bus.

Image Description: A White woman wearing sunglasses and a blond toddler wait in the shade of a bus shelter. A stroller with a white cane resting on it is next to the woman.

Acknowledgments

The heart of this book are the experiences that nondrivers shared with me. And while I made sure to compensate those I interviewed for this book, my initial list of interviewees was way too long. I couldn't include by name everyone whose knowledge and expertise informs this work, but it is the foundation of this work. I am deeply grateful for everyone who shared their story with me during my organizing work at Disability Rights Washington and for the support from the leadership of Disability Rights Washington, Mark Stroh and David Carlson, for allowing me the freedom to do this work, especially since I didn't have any other models of success to point to.

Going further back, this book, and the work that led to it, was only possible because of the years I spent learning how to organize while working for labor unions—especially from my first boss and mentor, Roxana Rivera. It was also shaped by the years I spent working with the American Civil Liberties Union and the communicators there, like my boss Paul Cates, who taught me how to think about the importance of finding the right stories to shift public opinion.

I also want to thank everyone who had patience for me as I figured out how to write a book, especially my editor, Heather Boyer, who held my hand through many, many versions of this book proposal. And finally, to my partner, who took over all the kid care when I took off, whether for a couple of hours or even sometimes a week, to get the space I needed to be able to write.

Despite What You Think, Not Everyone Drives

ONE-THIRD OF PEOPLE LIVING IN THE UNITED STATES don't have a driver's license.[1] This includes people like me who cannot drive because of a disability. It also includes young people, immigrants, people with suspended licenses, and people who have aged out of driving. Additionally, there are many people with licenses who can't afford to own a car or pay for insurance, parking, or gas. But because of who the majority of nondrivers are—disabled and poor people, unhoused or recently incarcerated individuals, undocumented immigrants, kids, young people, seniors aging out of driving—we are largely invisible, far from power structures that would enable us to create a world that could better meet our needs. The consequence of this invisibility is a mobility system designed almost exclusively for drivers. And that system has costs, not just for those of us excluded from it.

The truth is, car-dependent communities aren't just failing those of us who can't drive, they are failing everyone. They fail all of us by forcing us to make the land use decisions that drive up housing costs and saddle us with the financial burden of owning, operating, and maintaining a vehicle. Car dependency contributes to the public health crises of air and noise pollution and traffic crashes that cause life-changing injuries or deaths, all of which disproportionately harm low-income, Black, Brown, immigrant, and Native American communities. And perhaps most menacing of all, transportation is the leading contributor to carbon emissions. If we're serious about addressing climate change, we have to address our transportation system.

When I share the fact that a third of people in the United States can't, or can't afford to, drive, usually my audience is incredulous. Even among professionals in the transportation field, it's rare that someone grasps how many people are so profoundly excluded, if not severely limited, by not being able to grab car keys and go.

The narrative that everyone in the United States drives both shapes and is shaped by the metrics we use to try to understand mobility. How do we count who is a nondriver, not only those who can't physically drive, but also people who can't afford to drive or who don't have reliable access to a vehicle?

The metric I cite at the beginning of this chapter, that one-third of the people in this country can't drive, refers to the number of people in the United States without a valid driver's license.[2] But a driver's license is a crude measure of access to driving. For example, many seniors who lose the ability to drive still have a valid driver's license, and some people may retain a driver's license even while having a temporary disability that prevents them from driving. On the flip side, some people drive without a valid license, though that ability to drive comes with the risk of arrest.

Another metric used to measure transportation access is household vehicle ownership. Seven percent of American households do not own a car, and an additional 17 percent of households have a "vehicle deficit," meaning they have more adults than vehicles.[3] The Census asks about vehicle ownership in order to "plan and fund improvements to road and highway infrastructure" and "develop transportation plans and services."[4] But this is also an insufficient measurement of who has reliable access to a vehicle and the ability to drive it. Without understanding who within a household has primary access to a vehicle and the ability to drive, we can't understand disparities of access within households. For example, if a household has one vehicle that is used for one person to go to work, what kind of access do other household members have?

As part of my work in transportation advocacy at Disability Rights Washington, we and our allies successfully advocated for the state to fund a study on the demographics and mobility needs of nondrivers. The study was conducted by Toole Design in partnership with Cascadia Consulting and Strategic Research Associates and released in 2023. Using US Census Bureau and Federal Highway Administration Highway Statistics data, the study estimated that Washington's nondrivers represent 30 percent of our state population. These are people who are either under the age of 16 (and not eligible for a driver's license) or who are 16 or older and either do not have a driver's license or do not have a car.

In addition to the data analysis, the project team conducted a market research survey in which they called over fifty thousand phone numbers and reached out to 100,000 people online and asked them screening questions to identify nondrivers. Of those who were contacted, 2,786 met the screening criteria of being a nondriver, were over the age of 18, and responded to the survey. The respondents were from a geographically representative sample of the population of Washington State.[5]

Among people with driver's licenses and vehicles in their households who responded to the survey, "women, those under 25, and those with annual income under $56,000 are less likely to be the primary driver than males, those 25 years old and older, and those with income over $56,000."[6] By assuming that vehicle access among a household is equally distributed, the mobility needs of women, younger, and poorer individuals may not be evident.

Transportation mode is another common way to analyze how many people are drivers, but too often non-driving modes are undercounted when multiple modes are used on a single trip. Todd Litman from Victoria Transport Policy Institute writes that "commonly cited travel statistics, such as commute mode share, undercount active trips by ignoring shorter trips, non-commute trips, children's travel, recreational travel, and active links of trips that include motor vehicle travel. For example, a bike-transit-walk trip is often classified simply as a transit trip, and trips between parked vehicles and destinations are ignored even if they involve several blocks of walking."[7] Metrics that try to establish destination type or trip purpose struggle with how to measure these "chained" trips, which are more likely to be taken by caregivers, whose mobility needs have been historically ignored.

Technology to measure car traffic volumes is in use in most cities, but pedestrian and bicycle counts have not been prioritized. Cell phone signals are used to determine car traffic volumes and retime "adaptive" traffic signals to minimize backups. But because the pace of bicycle and pedestrian travel is so much slower and varied, the same technology cannot be used to count cyclists and pedestrians and retime signals to value their wait times and crossing needs.[8] Even with better pedestrian or bike counts, this data must be interpreted with caution. For example, very few people may choose to make a risky and highly unpleasant highway crossing to get from their apartment complex to a convenience store, but that doesn't mean there's not latent demand. The Washington

State Department of Transportation explains in its active transportation plan:

> WSDOT and other transportation agencies have historically focused on actual counts for decision making. That method does not account for barriers or places where there is a lack of infrastructure; for example, the sidewalk ends and the only option is to walk in the travel lane so fewer people use that sidewalk. It also does not account for the level of traffic stress in a place that discourages people who would otherwise use active transportation. In other words, focusing on counts of people already moving through a place does not account for the people who would be there if adequate facilities were provided.[9]

Alix Gould-Werth from the Washington Center for Equitable Growth and Dr. Alexandra Murphy, assistant professor of sociology at the University of Michigan, created a quantifiable metric for transportation that isn't focused on mode or trip purpose but rather on whether someone can get to the places they need to go in a safe or timely manner. The sixteen-question Transportation Security Index (TSI) is a valuable tool because it can provide data that measures transportation insecurity within households or between individuals who live on the same block. For instance, for someone who can drive, bike, or walk to the bus easily, a neighborhood might feel like it has good accessibility, but someone else who perhaps walks more slowly or doesn't feel safe waiting at a particular bus stop might not experience the same accessibility even though they live in the same household.[10]

When Gould-Werth and Murphy administered the TSI to a nationally representative sample of 1,999 adults in 2018, the researchers found that 1 out of 4 adults in the United States is transportation insecure. Fully half of adults experiencing poverty lacked transportation security, and Black and Hispanic adults were more likely to be transportation insecure than White adults.[11]

The Transportation Security Index is a powerful metric, not only because it allows us to look at transportation access for the individual, a more detailed measure than household or census block, but also because it expresses transportation access with more nuance and is able to reflect how disability, income, and social networks may be just as important to access as geography, transit service, and physical infrastructure.

So, while I refer to "nondrivers" in this book, I understand that this isn't always a strict binary between being able to drive and not being able to drive, having a functioning vehicle or not being able to pay for the needed repairs until the next paycheck. Driving access may be transitory, and even among people like me who have disabilities that fully prevent us from driving, our transportation access will vary depending on financial resources and stability, race, language proficiency, immigration status, gender, caregiving responsibilities, and geography.

But in a culture of car dependency, where our communities are almost always entirely built around vehicle mobility and speed, I think the binary of driver/nondriver is useful both in understanding access needs and in creating a cohesive political identity around which to mobilize for change. The fact that we have such insufficient knowledge of how people get around without driving, and how many of us and how frequently we travel or need to travel without driving ourselves, emphasizes how much this frame is needed.

We need to build a broad coalition, starting with nondrivers, to demand a different transportation and land use paradigm. This could be a powerful coalition given that car dependency is harming our public health and climate future. It could include advocates who want streets where children can safely navigate to the park or school, people who want to undo the harms of structural racism in highway construction, and those who want to reduce carbon emissions, connect rural and tribal communities to transit and multiuse trails, and create abundant affordable housing in places where it is possible to get around without a car.

Why This Book?

I want to be clear that while I center disability and accessibility throughout this book, this is not a book about disability and transportation. Some disabled people do drive, and for some disabled people, driving is the most accessible form of transportation. I'm interested in describing a different collective experience, the experience of not reliably being able to depend on driving for access in a society based on cars.

What does it mean that we have designed a transportation system that doesn't serve so many of us, and how can we change it? Nondrivers are a diverse group—from disabled people who can't drive because of our disabilities, to low-income, Black, Brown, Native American, and immigrant communities, to seniors aging out of driving and young people too young to drive or choosing to delay the costs of car ownership. But even with these differences, I'll discuss how our mobility needs form a cohesive identity.

When talking about disabled people, throughout this book I use "identity-first" language instead of "person-first" language. For example, instead of saying "I am a person with disabilities," I lead with the disability: "I am a disabled person." I made this choice because it's how I, as a low-vision person, choose to identify, and it is more consistent with how we talk about other parts of our identities. I wouldn't say that I am a person with queerness, or a person with Whiteness, for example. I recognize that other people prefer person-first language and that for many disabled people who for decades have fought to be recognized as deserving of the same respect as everyone else, person-first language is an important step toward recognizing that someone is not defined by their disability. So, if an interviewee expressed this preference, I honor that preference.

Using examples from our success in Washington State, I show how advocates working on climate change, safer roadways, environmental justice, and better transit and bike infrastructure can benefit from more intentionally seeking out collaboration with and leadership from involuntary nondrivers—people who can't drive or can't afford to—and how organizing across communities and across identities, we build bigger coalitions with more power.

Drawing from interviews with involuntary nondrivers from around the United States and from my own experience, I explain how nondrivers get around and the changes necessary to make our communities more accessible. These include sidewalk connectivity; reliable transit and paratransit; options for biking, scooting, and rolling; affordable and accessible housing; and the unrecognized burden of asking and paying for rides.

If there's one thing that you take from this book, I hope that it is the importance of listening to the knowledge of those who day in and day out rely on our network of sidewalks, on buses and paratransit, on rolling or biking, or on asking and paying others for rides. It is critical to include involuntary nondrivers in transportation planning decisions. I outline steps organizations can take to include and promote leadership of those who are most impacted—and too often excluded—by transportation systems designed and run by people with driving privilege. And if you don't work for an organization in the transportation or land use space, I've included a checklist of actions you, as an individual living in a car-dependent society, can take in your own life to help all of us move beyond automobility.

When the needs of involuntary nondrivers are viewed as essential to how we design our transportation systems and our communities, not only will we be able to more easily get where *we* need to go, but the changes will lead to healthier, climate-friendly communities for everyone. So, what are we waiting for?

CHAPTER 1

Nondrivers Are Everywhere

WHAT ARE THE REASONS PEOPLE DON'T OR CAN'T DRIVE? How many people don't drive as a lifestyle choice versus an economic necessity?

In the survey of adult nondrivers commissioned by the Washington State legislature and described in the introduction, 68 percent of respondents listed the cost of purchasing, operating, or insuring a vehicle as the barrier to driving. Nineteen percent of respondents said they couldn't drive because of a disability, and 14 percent because they didn't know how to drive or couldn't afford to get a driver's license. Seventeen percent of respondents reported that they preferred a lifestyle without a car, and 17 percent of respondents wrote in other reasons, like suspended licenses, anxiety around driving, or that someone else in their household uses the car.[1]

The "choice" nondrivers—people who have the financial resources, immigration status, and physical ability to own and drive a vehicle but choose not to—were more likely to be "male, younger, urban, and higher income."[2] This tracks with who people often think of as nondrivers, the urbanist, White, male, nondisabled, and financially stable voices that tend to dominate bike advocacy, transit nerd, and city planning spaces. With the invisibility of involuntary nondrivers, advocacy priorities fail to address the needs of those of us who can't drive or can't afford to.

The expertise and the lived experience that I highlight in this book comes from involuntary nondrivers, with an emphasis on the expertise of low-income, Black, Brown, immigrant, and disabled people, caregivers, and queer and trans people. Our exclusion from a world built around automobility means that we are deeply vested in rethinking car dependency, but because of poverty, racism, and caregiving responsibilities, ableism and language barriers, homophobia, transphobia, ageism, and long work hours, we continue to be largely invisible in the rooms where transportation priorities get set.

I recognize that many of you reading this book are likely choice nondrivers, or possibly drivers, who want to see more transit, walking, rolling, and riding mobility options available in your community. That's great! We welcome you as part of the nondriver movement! Because the changes we need to move away from car dependency will require the biggest, broadest coalition of allies we can convene. While you may not see your experiences reflected in this book, my hope is that by understanding the experiences of other nondrivers, you will become more dedicated to fighting for the changes we *all* need.

This chapter explores the different reasons *why* people are nondrivers—whether it's because of a disability, age, documentation status, poverty, or racist enforcement systems. And while I have separated these into subsections, it's critical to understand that these categories overlap and intersect. While someone might not be able to drive because of a disability, their experience of mobility if they're a White, middle-class, disabled person will be very different than if they are disabled, Black, and poor. And while I touch on age, race, and immigration status, others have far deeper personal and professional expertise in these areas, and I encourage the reader to go deeper with the work I reference in these sections.

The stories and identities described in this chapter do not make up an exhaustive list of nondrivers. Every time I interview someone for our storymap project for Disability Rights Washington, their experience reinforces how many different ways people experience access and mobility and how that can be shaped by their identities, their wealth, their social networks, and the geography and resources of the communities in which they live. While there is no way for me to capture all this nuance in one chapter, my intention is for you to start to understand how many involuntary nondrivers are out there, in your town, on your street, and even within your own family and the reasons that communities built around driving cannot or do not serve our needs.

Nondrivers are Disabled

If you ask someone from the United States what image comes to mind when they think about disability, it's probably a disabled parking spot sign. These signs with a stick figure in a wheelchair are probably the most, if not the only, visible manifestation of disability in many public spaces. But the reality is that many disabled people can't drive or can't afford cars. People with disabilities are four times less likely to drive than nondisabled people, and two to three times more likely to live in a zero-vehicle household. We use buses, subways, and commuter rail for a higher share of trips than people without disabilities.[3]

There are many kinds of disabilities that can make driving impossible or unsafe. Some disabled people may be able to drive if they can afford a costly adaptive vehicle, but because many disabled people are unemployed or underemployed and live in poverty, even if their disability doesn't prevent them from driving, they may not be able to afford a vehicle. According to the Center for American Progress, disabled adults are twice as likely to experience poverty as their nondisabled peers.[4]

Because mobility in the United States is largely based around the ability to drive, this disparity results in far fewer opportunities for disabled people to participate in their communities. In a 2001 study by the Urban Institute, 29 percent of workers with disabilities cited transportation as a barrier to employment.[5] In 2021, the Department of Labor reported that for working-age people receiving disability payments, 51 percent of people who couldn't drive said transportation prevented them from working, compared to only 31 percent of people who could drive.[6] Lack of access is one of the factors contributing to much lower employment rates for disabled people. The Center for American Progress reports that in 2021, nondisabled workers were three times more likely than disabled workers to be employed.[7]

And while many nondrivers are disabled, many are not, or would not choose to identify as disabled, even though they may have physical or mental health conditions that prevent them from driving.

"Many people who may have health conditions or who would otherwise be covered under the ADA do not identify as disabled," explains Carol Tyson, the government affairs liaison for the Disability Rights and Education Defense Fund (DREDF) and current chair of the Consortium for Constituents with Disabilities. "Older adults who age into disability, those who acquire a disability, and even those with lifelong conditions might not identify [as disabled] because of the continued stigma attached to being disabled, cultural differences, or not feeling reflected or comfortable in often majority-White disability rights' spaces."

Especially for people who do not present as disabled and people with so called "invisible disabilities," masking can feel like a wise choice. Devin Silvernail is a father and a nondriver who lives in Seattle. Like me, he has nystagmus and doesn't see well enough to drive. Until recently, Silvernail didn't want to disclose that he couldn't drive because of his vision. Instead, he would tell people he didn't have a car for environmental reasons.

"It was something that I always tried to hide," Silvernail told me. "We were trained to believe that it was a bad thing, like it was shameful that you couldn't drive, so I hid my disability from girlfriends, from coworkers, from people I met on the street."

For other disabled people, masking is not an option. Kimberly Glass was born with osteogenesis imperfecta, a congenital disability that causes brittle bones. Glass could drive with an assistive setup and modifications, but that setup costs upward of $60,000, far beyond her budget as someone living on disability income. She relies on the paratransit system in Reno, Nevada, but the unreliability of the system has really limited her ability to get to work or to take her daughter to activities, even things as basic as doctor's appointments. "I've lost jobs because I couldn't get there on time. People forget that just because we're disabled, that doesn't mean we don't have a life and children and families and things to do," Glass shared.

Glass's experience is not unique. For Erica Jones, who uses a battery-powered electric wheelchair (often called a powerchair), the cost of a wheelchair-accessible vehicle is prohibitive.

"I do sometimes use a personal car, but a lot of the time I can't," Jones explains. "Because of the nature of my disabilities, I need a heavy motorized wheelchair to get around. And that unfortunately does not fit in my personal vehicle." If she drives somewhere in her car, Jones can't get out, which limits her to drive-through or curbside services. As a result, she primarily uses the bus and light-rail to go places.

For people with chronic health conditions who experience flare-ups or have limited energy, driving can be feasible on some days and in some situations, but not in others. Grace Hope's chronic health condition meant they had to stop driving approximately eight years ago, after they lost "pretty significant" use of their hands. When they first lost the ability to drive, Hope was married and relied a lot on their partner for rides. "Once I went through my divorce about five years ago, it meant being a single parent who didn't have the ability to drive," Hope shared.

When their condition improved last year, Hope felt like they might be able to start driving again, so they bought a vehicle, but they quickly discovered that they couldn't safely drive on the freeway, and on some days they can't drive at all. On "good" days, though, Hope is able to drive short distances around town, which has greatly improved their commute time into their job in Seattle. Commuting by bus could take five hours a day, but when Hope can drive to the regional transit center to catch an express bus, their daily commute only takes two hours and forty-five minutes.

These stories show that having access to a vehicle doesn't always result in being able to drive regularly. A 2022 report from the Bureau of Transportation Statistics shows that just over 60 percent of disabled people with cars drive them on a regular basis, compared to nearly 92 percent of nondisabled respondents.[8]

Other disabled people have mobility disabilities that prevent them from driving, regardless of the vehicle setup. Tanisha Sepúlveda is a powerchair user from Seattle who has a spinal cord injury and owns a wheelchair-accessible van, but because she cannot drive, she relies on her partner to drive her in it. When her partner isn't able, Sepúlveda takes the bus.

"It is a sense of freedom being able to pick up and go wherever, whenever you want," Sepúlveda reflected on her time as a driver.

Sepúlveda felt fortunate that she was living in Seattle and relying on transit before her injury. If she'd been living in Hot Springs, Arkansas, where she grew up, the lack of public transit options would have made her mobility much more challenging. "I was really surprised at the independence I still felt with Seattle public transportation," she said.

But with the rapid increase in Seattle rents, she was forced to move farther out. Sepúlveda now lives in Delridge, a historically redlined part of the city, where sidewalk connectivity is not as good as it is in downtown Seattle. As a result, she finds herself rolling in the street when curb ramps are missing or sidewalks aren't in good repair.

Some disabled people stop driving when a neurological condition like ALS, multiple sclerosis, or epilepsy means that it's no longer a safe option, or after a stroke or brain injury. Harry Kiick has had a seizure disorder his whole life, and for many years he drove. He knew it wasn't ideal, but he thought he didn't have a choice. In 1995, "I had a terrible accident that was caused by a seizure," shared Kiick. "I totaled the car, spent a week in the hospital, almost drove through somebody's living room. I decided, no, I shouldn't be doing this, obviously this condition was worse than I thought it was. Luckily, I only hurt myself and not anyone else, so I didn't have to live with that." Kiick now relies on transit and has become a member of the citizens advisory committee for his regional transit agency.

Many disabled nondrivers are people like me whose vision doesn't allow us to drive safely. Researchers estimate that 3.2 million people in the United States are low vision or legally blind. Legally blind means having corrected vision of less than 20/100, meaning that even with glasses you see less than 20/100 on a vision chart. Low-vision people have corrected vision between 20/40 and 20/100.

While requirements vary from state to state, many states require at least 20/40 vision to pass a driver's license test. Sometimes, if a low-vision person is close to passing the DMV vision test, they can get a restricted license that allows them to drive only on local roads during daylight hours. Some states permit vision scopes and other aids that can help low-vision drivers to read signs.[9] For myself, and for many other low-vision people I've spoken to, the fear of causing serious injury or death because we didn't see something keeps us from seriously considering attempting to qualify for these restricted licenses.

Driving isn't a possibility for the more than one million people in the United States who are legally blind. Among working-age adults, vision loss from diabetes is the leading cause of blindness,[10] and there is a higher risk of vision loss among people who are Black and/or Latino than people who are White.[11]

As an adult, Teaera Turner lost her vision from diabetes. Like many people who lose their vision as adults, Turner participated in an orientation and mobility training to learn blindness skills, including how to use a white cane to safely navigate sidewalks, cross streets, and use public transit. But for Turner, getting from her home to the nearby light-rail station still feels too dangerous because it requires crossing high-speed roads. So, she must pre-schedule and wait for paratransit rides.

"I miss so much about driving," Turner reflected. "Not having to wait for somebody to get you, not having to be on somebody else's time, arriving just when you want to arrive somewhere because you can do the timing and map things out yourself."

Less visible, and less widely discussed, is when anxiety or mental health conditions keep people from driving. Melanie Perry lives in Spokane, and she normally gets around by the bus, but she also bikes or walks shorter distances in nicer weather. She has tried to get a driver's license a few times but never felt comfortable enough to take the test. "It was anxiety and depression that prevented me from getting to the point of taking the driver's test. And my mom's anxiety made it difficult for her to teach me," Perry shared.

Neurodivergent people may also experience difficulty driving. Noor Pervez, the community engagement manager for the Autistic Self Advocacy Network (ASAN), explains that overstimulation can be a significant barrier: "Particularly with a new generation of cars, the LED lights are so much brighter than the previous versions. It's not the best thing for all types of brains." While some people with autism can drive, and some may find driving to be more accessible than relying on transit or rideshare, for other neurodivergent people, driving is not an option.

Nondrivers Can't Afford to Drive

Pervez emphasized how many neurodiverse people don't drive simply because they can't afford to: "A lot of people, even among the relatively low statistically amount of us that are employed and not underemployed, can't afford a car. Those of us that can afford a car usually can't afford a new one, a lot of us can't afford upkeep and maintenance." And the cost of owning a car doubles or triples if you need a powerchair van or other adaptive vehicle, he added, and gets even more complicated if you live in a more rural area where getting an adaptive vehicle serviced is near impossible.

Black disabled Americans are more likely to live in poverty than their White disabled peers. The Century Foundation reported that in 2020 one in four disabled Black adults lived in poverty compared to just over one in seven of their White counterparts. And this disparity hasn't narrowed much in recent years. "The Black-White poverty gap among working-age people with disabilities was only 1.6 percentage points smaller in 2020 than it was in 2013," the report notes.[12]

Many people who are disabled must remain in poverty in order to qualify for needed health care or home care support, support services that wouldn't be covered even with "good" health care coverage from an employer. Tamara Jackson, a policy analyst for the Wisconsin Board for People with Developmental Disabilities and co-chair of the Wisconsin Non-Driver Advisory Committee, explains: "The reality is that you have a system where pre-poverty is a prerequisite." A 2020 report on employment and disability from the National Council on Disability describes this "poverty trap," explaining that many disabled people "agonize over the choice between maintaining the health care that they need to live and work, or a job that they are qualified for and desire, given the asset limitations imposed by means-tested programs that are attached to health care."[13]

Of course, it's not only disabled people who can't afford to drive. In a 2011 report, the Bureau of Transportation Statistics found that low-income households earning under $25,000 are nine times less likely to own a car than households earning more than $25,000.[14] A lack of transportation access further limits opportunities to earn money.

In the survey of Washington State nondrivers, when asked why they did not drive, cost was the most frequently cited barrier: "Forty percent said the costs of purchasing, operating, and maintaining a vehicle are too high, while another 28 percent stated that the costs of vehicle registration and insurance are too high."

The researchers found that more than 40 percent of nondriver survey respondents had an annual household income of less than $28,000. Of the total Washington State population, only 15 percent of households make less than $25,000 a year. The survey also found that 53 percent of survey respondents rent a house or apartment compared to 37 percent of the Washington State population who rent a house or apartment.

Nondrivers Are Black, Native American, and Native Alaskan

Using 2019 data, the National Equity Atlas found that 18 percent of Black households lacked access to a vehicle, compared to only 6 percent of White households.[15] In Washington State, while African Americans make up 4 percent of the state population, 9 percent of the nondriver survey respondents identified as African American. And Native Americans make up 1 percent of the state population, yet 7 percent of the nondriver survey respondents said they are Native American.[16] According to the Equity Atlas, 48 percent of Native American and Native Alaskan households lack access to a vehicle, and a 2016 study found that close to a third of households participating in the federal food assistance program on reservations lacked access to a vehicle.[17]

The racial disparities in household vehicle access, which hold constant in both more urbanized and more rural states, are a result of the racial wealth gap and the high cost of vehicle ownership. The disparities are exacerbated by the fact that auto loans and car insurance are often more expensive for Black and Hispanic/Latino owners, even when controlled for credit scores.[18]

Black drivers are also more likely to be pulled over in discretionary traffic stops, resulting in compounding court fines and fees and the potential for license suspension. More than half the states in the US still allow license suspensions for unpaid fines and fees,[19] and a study that examined data from New Jersey found nondriving-related suspensions to be seven times more likely in low-income, as compared to high-income, census tracts.[20] In Washington State, around 4 percent of driver's licenses were suspended in 2022;[21] nationally, 2.59 percent of licenses are suspended, though the rates of license suspensions in some cities are over 10 percent.[22]

As a White person, I have not experienced the kind of "arrested mobility," that Charles T. Brown describes in his work on the policing of the movement of Black and Brown people. Brown's podcast, research, and educational resources describe the ways enforcement and race interact and create inequitable, and often dangerous or deadly, outcomes.[23] Sara A. Seo's *Policing the Open Road: How Cars Transformed American Freedom* offers a legal history of the policing of automobility and is also helpful in understanding racist policing practices that underpin so much of how we conceptualize road safety.[24]

I had a small window into the intersection of policing and mobility when, in 2016, I worked on a contract for the American Civil Liberties Union to investigate if courts in and around the Memphis area were acting as debtors' prisons: booking people in jail when they showed up for court dates if they couldn't pay fines or fees associated with court costs. I spent a week observing court proceedings in Memphis, where most of the cases involved minor traffic infractions, such as broken taillights, missing tags, tinted windows, or not using a seatbelt. Aside from the judges, pro-bono lawyers, and court staff, I was the only White person I saw in court.

"They pull you over for anything—they claim they can't see your tags, and it's just the angle they were looking at your car," one of the plaintiffs, a young mother, told me. She had received a citation for improperly displayed tags, and the compounding fines and fees and missed court dates resulted in her license being suspended. She was in court that day to try to get her license restored, but the compounding court fees and fines meant she wasn't going to be able to pay off the debt. Like many of the other people in court that day, she would continue to drive without a valid license and risk being arrested again, because without driving, she wouldn't be able to work or get her kids where they need to go.

Nondrivers Are Immigrants

Because most states require valid immigration documentation to receive a driver's license, undocumented immigrants often cannot legally drive in the US. Fortunately, eighteen states and the District of Columbia have enacted laws that allow people without legal US residency to apply for a driver's license by showing identification from their country of origin.[25] In 2013 California was the first state to pass this type of legislation.[26] But for immigrants who worry about having their home address and photo in a government database, driving without documentation may feel safer, especially in states where the driver's licenses databases are searchable by Immigration and Customs Enforcement (ICE).[27] For many, riding public transit, biking, walking, or relying on friends and family for rides feels like the safest option.

Even for immigrants with documentation or the ability to get a driver's license, the cost of car ownership can be a burden. The National Equity Atlas notes that "immigrant households for all racial and ethnic groups, except Black households, are more likely to lack access to a vehicle compared to their US-born counterparts."[28] Low-income immigrants have to make difficult choices between car ownership and affording other essentials. Because we have made driving a prerequisite for employment and full community participation in so many parts of our country, too often this doesn't feel like a choice.

In interviewing nondrivers in Washington State for our story-map project, I partnered with Living Well Kent, a nonprofit serving Iraqi and Afghani families resettled in the Kent area, a suburb south of Seattle. Rajwinder, Khadija, and Nabaa are all mothers and were recent immigrants when I met them through this program.

"Availability of public transportation in the area is one of the biggest barriers as there are not many bus services," Rajwinder shared. "A lot of the routes have been cut so I must walk long distances to catch multiple different buses to get to a destination. Sometimes I get late because of routes changing and I have to walk for too long and miss the bus."[29]

Where bus service does exist, the low frequency of service makes it far less convenient than driving. Bus stops can be far apart and often lack shelters. King County Metro conducted an equity analysis of existing transit service in 2020 and identified the parts of Kent and Auburn where many immigrant families live as areas of high unmet need. Although the areas are high density, home to "a high proportion of low-income people, people of color, people with disabilities, and members of limited-English speaking communities," they have "limited mid-day and evening transit service to schools, jobs, and childcare centers and other ways to build wealth and opportunities."[30]

Relying on transit here can be particularly difficult when waiting with children, as Khadija pointed out: "We wait for a long time, sometimes it rains, sometimes it's sunny. It's not great for the kids because of the conditions." And for some, language barriers and understanding how to navigate a new community on the bus is extremely stressful. For many families, saving to afford a car and getting US driver's licenses is an immediate priority, though when a family can afford only one car, access must be negotiated. Nabaa described feeling frustrated about having to rely on her husband to drive: "Always my husband driving me and my kids—to school, to shopping, to have fun outside, to the park—anything."

When our communities are designed to work best for, and only for, car-based mobility, the cost of not driving is unemployment and foregoing basic needs. So, people will choose to buy and maintain a vehicle, despite it being a significant financial burden and stressor.

It's also important to remember that many disabled people rely on low-wage and immigrant workers who serve as caregivers, personal care attendants, or direct service providers. These service providers often allow people to remain in their own homes with their family and loved ones instead of in an institution. Before their work in disability advocacy, Carol Tyson from DREDF spent decades working for economic justice and worker rights. They offer the reminder that the mobility of disabled people is dependent on the mobility of the caregivers and service providers many disabled people rely on to live in the community. "Caregivers are often low income or a recent immigrant and may not have access to a car," they shared.

Nondrivers Are Seniors

Most driving adults don't want to consider this, but on average, Americans will spend the last seven to ten years of their life unable to safely drive.[31] Danielle Arigoni, author of *Climate Resilience for an Aging Nation*, notes that 18 percent of people 65 and older don't drive.[32] Arigoni points out that while people can make modifications inside their home to accommodate changing needs, "it's much more difficult to jump into and instantly modify your transportation opportunities if you don't live in a walkable or bikeable community, or if you don't live near public transit."

And we know that our population is aging: the AARP Livable Communities initiative states that by 2034, for the first time, the United States' population will have more older adults than children.[33] In fact, the number of potential drivers over the age of 65 will increase 77 percent by 2045.[34] But instead of ensuring that seniors can transition to walkable, rollable, and transit-rich living situations, it is far more common to move them into assisted living facilities that may provide some group transportation options, but not a connected sidewalk network or easy access to public transit options that would make independent mobility possible.

Arigoni emphasizes the importance of building more housing in proximity to transit, housing that's well supported by bike and pedestrian infrastructure. Because housing in urban areas is so expensive, for many seniors, it may not be possible to afford housing that is well served by transit or in walkable communities. Roughly 12 percent of older adults rely on Social Security payments alone, and half of older people who live alone are struggling to get by on less than $27,000 a year.[35]

Too often, affordable communities for retirees are farther from urban centers with health care facilities or reliable transit, and so service to more rural areas, even if it's only once a day or runs only a few days a week, can be a lifeline.

After she lost much of her vision, Nancy Perron, who raised her family and then retired in a rural river valley outside of Aberdeen, Washington, had to stop driving. (Yes, the Aberdeen where Kurt

Cobain grew up, which continues to be one of the poorest cities in the state after the lumber industry began to collapse in the 1980s.) Perron had no desire to move into the city, having a strong network of family members nearby. "I can tell you that moving to town is not an option for most of us that live in the country," Perron said, explaining that expecting individuals to move from their communities and networks of support was "putting the responsibility for a community service on one individual." Also, she added, "for the average person living on Social Security, you don't just get to move around." She knew she couldn't afford a place in town, and also knew that the waiting list for Section 8 housing opened up so infrequently that she was unlikely to ever get a spot.

But then the bus route that served the valley where she lived was reduced due to funding cuts. Perron had worked as the deputy county coroner and had seen what could happen when older adults lost transportation in rural areas. "When you go to people's houses where they've been isolated for too long, it's not a healthy situation whatsoever. We shouldn't be making choices for other people, but we should make sure they can make their own choices and get out of there, go to town, get food instead of eating the cat food or the dog food, which I have seen," Perron insists.

Luckily, Perron was able to convince the local paratransit agency to continue to offer service to her family and so she's been able to remain in her home, but she worries every year as transit budgets are stretched and routes reorganized that she could lose this critical service.

For some seniors, especially people diagnosed with progressive chronic health conditions, and with the resources to move, planning for a future where they can't drive is critical. This is a strategy Arigoni endorses. By moving into housing with more transportation options before they can no longer drive, seniors can build new "transportation muscle memories" and learn how to use alternatives before they lose the ability to drive.

When John Frasca retired and moved to the coastal community of Port Townsend, Washington, he sought out a home with a bus stop close by. He has ALS, and as it progressed, Frasca stopped driving. He's more limited now that he can't pop out quickly and drive to the grocery store because he forgot an ingredient for dinner, but he is able to live independently. (Although he can no longer drive, Frasca still has a valid driver's license, which he uses for identification, so in estimations of drivers based on license status, he would still be counted.)

"I have been a strong proponent of bus transportation and was happy to find that Port Townsend has a system that works for me," Frasca shares. "I am grateful for the Dial-A-Ride paratransit service provided by Jefferson Transit, and I rely on that to get to local medical appointments and events that are beyond the range of my power wheelchair."

Not too far from Frasca's condominium, Port Angeles Councilmember Lindsey Schromen-Wawrin has noted this incongruence: "On the Olympic Peninsula, a lot of people move here and retire here. Why would we be building car-dependent urban spaces, when we shouldn't expect people to drive as they become elders? And so, we're not really creating a space that's accessible for people, whether they're older, or whether they're younger. And that's really, I think, a disservice to our population as a whole."[36]

But for many seniors, it's too difficult to imagine a future without driving, and the stigma around identifying as disabled or admitting they can no longer drive is a barrier to action. In their survey of nondrivers in Washington State, researchers found that "senior nondrivers were more likely to have a driver's license and more likely to have a vehicle in their household compared to the nondriver survey respondents under 64 years old."[37]

The researchers noted that they likely undersampled older non-drivers in their survey: "While the screening criteria sought to capture the group of older adults that have a driver license and primary access to a vehicle, but do not drive most places, the low response rate for phone surveys (yet high rate of older adults that took the phone survey versus the online survey) indicates there may have been a difficulty in either reaching older adults that met the criteria or controlling for responses on this topic that can be one of frustration and anxiety for older adults."

For many, raised in our culture of ableism, there are deep fears about what it means to get older and to lose the ability to do things independently. But not being able to drive shouldn't have to limit the ability to participate in your community. It is important to normalize nondriving so that we can start building communities that work better for everyone, including the increasing number of seniors who cannot safely drive themselves.

Nondrivers Are Children and Youth

The largest segment of nondrivers are children. Almost 20 percent of US residents are 15 or younger.[38] I often get pushback about counting children as nondrivers. Because children can't travel independently, they shouldn't count, I often hear. But I disagree fundamentally.

First, because many children can and do travel independently, and in the right environments, children don't need to be accompanied by adults for every trip. In Japan, as evident in the much-discussed Japanese reality TV show *Old Enough*, young children safely navigate streets that are designed for slower car speeds. And while allowing children to ride public transit by themselves may seem unreasonable in many middle-class, suburban communities, in New York City, many schoolchildren ride the subway or public bus on their own for transportation by seventh grade.[39]

More importantly, whether or not someone can make every trip by themselves, mobility should not be tied to whether someone has the ability to travel independently. For some disabled adults with cognitive disabilities or who need support from a health care aid, traveling alone may not be safe or practical.

No matter your age, no matter your physical or cognitive access needs, you should have the right to be mobile and get to the places you need to be part of your community. Trying to draw a line between people "deserving" of mobility and those too young or "too disabled" to have this right only leads to unnecessary exclusion and ugly assumptions around whose life has value. No matter your age, whether or not you can travel by yourself, it can and should be possible to get to the places you need to go without driving.

"Transportation access underpins everything," reflects Judy Shanley, PhD, co-chair of the Transportation Research Board Committee on Accessible Transportation and Mobility. Shanley began her career as a special education teacher and helped youth with disabilities and their families to develop "transition plans" to identify the supports each student needs to move from high school into the workplace or to higher education. "If students, their families, and the transition professionals working with them don't think about transportation and mobility, student attainment of postschool goals will never be realized." At Easterseals, Shanley works with state educational agencies and school districts to identify transportation services to support student access to safe and reliable transportation services when they leave high school.

Additionally, when we design communities that require children to be driven, the burden of transporting children falls on caregivers, and not all caregivers have a vehicle, the ability to drive, or the schedule flexibility to provide transportation. It's why our public school systems so often provide transportation—because they recognize that without busing access, the families with the least resources or with caregivers who are nondrivers wouldn't be able to get their children to school.

According to the Bureau of Transportation Statistics, the majority of children from low-income families take the school bus. For families that are not low income, the majority of children are driven in a private vehicle.[40] But the school bus system is struggling to meet the mobility needs of students. A national bus driver shortage means that many districts are having difficulty serving routes. Busing is also expensive. Nationally, we spend $25 billion a year on school bus service.[41] In the city of Seattle, transportation costs are more than $3,000 per student annually.[42]

Facing budget shortfalls and driver shortages, many school districts are looking at how to make it safe and accessible for more children to walk, roll, or bike to school. Seattle started staggering start times between schools so the limited number of bus drivers can cover two routes.[43] Philadelphia is paying parents $300 per month to drive their own kids.[44] But since the 1970s, the rate of children walking, rolling, or biking to school has decreased from 50 percent in 1969 to 11 percent today.[45]

Kori Johnson, program and engagement manager at the Safe Routes Partnership, attributed some of these decreases to an increase in school choice, where students have the option to attend an out-of-boundary school instead of their neighborhood school. That means students might be traveling to schools that are far away from where they live. She also called out another major challenge in school siting, where often the most affordable land for schools is on the outskirts of communities or along major highways, where there's no way for students to walk or roll to campus.

"In the past, schools were nestled into walkable neighborhoods," Johnson said. "Today, a lot of schools that are being built are just not bikeable or walkable due to their location. They just find the largest and cheapest land—which is usually far away from residential neighborhoods and in less desirable industrial areas or areas off busy highways."

Many youth who are old enough and physically able to drive can't afford to drive or are electing not to take on the stress and cost of driving. In the early 2000s, there was a lot of reporting on how millennials weren't driving at the same rate as previous generations. We've seen a new round of similar stories about Gen Z. The *Washington Post* reported that in 2020, only 25 percent of 16-year-olds had driver's licenses in the United States, compared to 43 percent in 1997. The decrease in licenses for young adults was also notable: today only 80 percent of 20- to 25-year-olds have licenses, compared to 90 percent in 1997.[46] These changes could be due to a combination of increased online socialization options for youth, anxiety around the risks of driving, and the risk of encounters with police, especially for Black and Brown drivers.[47]

It is encouraging that getting a driver's license is less of a rite of passage culturally in the United States, and perhaps now viewed as something more akin to other adult responsibilities that are anxiety inducing and expensive, like finding your own health insurance coverage. And the increasingly real impacts of climate change motivate many young people to question whether they want to embrace car dependency.

Adah Crandall, a sixteen-year-old from Portland, Oregon, is questioning whether she wants to get a driver's license, even though she realizes having a license would give her more mobility options. With Sunrise Portland, Crandall has been organizing to stop a freeway expansion project that would worsen the air quality and increase the risk of traffic violence near her former middle school. She spoke about the climate impacts of highway expansion: "Forty percent of Oregon's reported carbon emissions come from transportation. People don't really think about freeways as a climate issue. And that is a very intentional move by the Department of Transportation. They are this secret climate villain that is hiding because people can't imagine a system where they're not driving everywhere every day all the time."

For Crandall, not getting a driver's license is a choice, but for many youth, the cost of driver's education, high insurance rates, and the cost of buying a car or paying for gas means that low-income and non-White teens are much less likely to drive than their affluent and White peers. With her research about the travel modes of youth, Rutgers professor Dr. Kelcie Ralph found "staggering differences in travel mode . . . young people were less likely to be Drivers and more likely to be Carless if they had relatively low household incomes or were a racial/ethnic minority (other than non-Hispanic Asian)."[48]

Micah Lusignan grew up in SeaTac in South King County, a working-class community near the Seattle airport, where almost half of all households speak a language other than English at home.[49] Lusignan lost his vision in middle school and will never be able to drive. But growing up in a low-income community, none of his peers could drive either. "Especially for the majority of my friends, coming from a lower-income community, many of us did not have access to cars," Lusignan shared. It was normal for everyone to get where they needed to go on the bus. Communities with robust transit networks and safe places to walk, roll, or bike can reduce the disparities between youth and children that have access to driving or being driven and those that do not.

The needs of young nondrivers are not less important than, or fundamentally different than, the needs of adult nondrivers. Acting as if children's mobility needs are nonexistent or somehow fundamentally different only serves to erase the mobility needs of adults who can't drive. Counting youth, and fully valuing their need for communities where they can get where they need to go safely and accessibly, with or without a caregiver or companion, can help us build the kind of broad coalition we need to undo car dependency.

CHAPTER 2

What Nondrivers Need

WHEN I WANT TO GO SOMEWHERE NEW, whether to a friend's house in a part of the city I don't know well, to a medical clinic in the region, or to another part of the state to interview a nondriver who wants to share their story, I have to set aside a decent chunk of time for planning.

Google Maps reminds me (as it has for years) that biking and walking directions are in beta mode and shouldn't be fully trusted. This is evident every time I try to use Google Maps to get a bike route in Seattle: it reliably directs me to a former state highway (and still a multilane, crash-prone speedway with no bike infrastructure) anytime I try to navigate from my home.

Google Maps and other mapping services like Transit App do a decent job of pulling transit routes and real-time schedules from the transit agencies that make the information available, but if I want to travel to a more rural part of my state, I need to dig around the local transit agency websites to find PDF route maps and schedules. If I want to figure out the best way to combine biking and transit, Google Maps is no help. Data about accessible sidewalks and crossings isn't available in Google Maps, and local mapping tools simply don't exist in most places.

It's not just the lack of information available to mapping programs that makes this difficult, it's that too often there just isn't a way to get there: gaps in the sidewalk network, nonexistent bike lanes or multiuse paths, transit routes that leave ten-mile gaps between one community and the next or that run only once a day. Or there may be a way to get where you need to go, but it involves unacceptable risks, like waiting ninety minutes at a lonely park and ride in the dark, or rolling down the side of a 50-miles-per-hour road where there's no shoulder or sidewalk.

People who can drive and have easy access to a car can plug an address into a mapping app, hit go, and not have to wonder if the roads will actually connect. We've spent a hundred years investing billions in easy, direct, and speedy access for cars, even revolutionizing housing, land use, and zoning patterns to prioritize car access and mobility.

In this chapter I describe the infrastructure and transportation services on which nondrivers rely and what we have to contend with when the infrastructure and mobility options available to us are not adequate—or not available at all. In a country where the distances we need to cover to meet basic needs have been elongated by automobility, it's important to consider how we can reduce the need to travel long distances to meet daily needs through denser and more integrated land use and the opportunity for remote access to some activities.

Nondrivers Rely on Sidewalks

Krystal Monteros was looking for an apartment in Tacoma, Washington. She liked her apartment and community in the suburb of University Place, but her landlord was no longer accepting her Section 8 vouchers. She knew that she probably wouldn't be able to find a place that was designed especially for wheelchair users with low kitchen shelves and accessible bathrooms, but she needed a place that was wheelchair accessible—located on the ground floor, without steps, and with doorways wide enough for her chair to fit through. And there weren't a lot of affordable options.

Tacoma, once the terminus of the first transnational rail connection to the Northwest, became the industrial hub of Puget Sound, with pulp and paper mills contributing the infamous "Tacoma Aroma." It remained Seattle's more affordable, working-class neighbor, but as the Seattle tech boom began in the 2010s, new demand for housing throughout the region drove up prices.

To find anything accessible that she could afford, Monteros had to look at apartment complexes in the neighboring exurban community of Lakewood. When Monteros rolled off the bus to go check out one of these listings, she was in for an unpleasant surprise. While the bus stop sat on a cement pad, it was surrounded by dirt. And the dirt path narrowed to less than a foot wide just south of the bus stop, squeezed between a fence and the four-lane suburban arterial with no shoulder. There was no way for Monteros to get to the entrance of the apartment complex where she might be able to rent. She waited for the next bus, rode it to the end of the line where it circled back, and went home.

Eventually, Monteros found an apartment across from the same bus stop, on the other side of the street. There's a sidewalk and a bus stop for northbound buses on that side, but when she is coming home, she still has to get off on the stop without sidewalks, and if it's been raining a lot, the section of dirt she has to traverse to get to the crosswalk will have turned to mud. "I literally have to have my neighbors come and help me get through this area that there's no sidewalk in," Monteros shares.

And it's not just this corner. A staggering 58 percent of arterials where she lives in Pierce County have no sidewalks.[1] Monteros often finds herself getting off a bus and getting stuck or stranded. Sometimes, she has to call her sister to drive over and help her get unstuck.

Planners may assume that people with mobility-limiting disabilities don't use walking or rolling to get where they need to go, but the inverse is true. According to the Bureau of Transportation Statistics, adults with disabilities who work walk or roll for a greater share of trips than workers without disabilities.[2]

Monteros returns to University Place where she used to live to do her shopping because she knows the sidewalk network is more accessible and reliable, and so she's less likely to find herself stuck. "Even though I don't even live in University Place, I choose to do all my grocery shopping and having my pharmacy and everything there. I will take a longer bus route just because it is so much easier for me to get around there," Monteros explains. "We need to start thinking about public transportation and sidewalks as going together instead of as two separate things. You can't use the bus if you can't get yourself to the bus stop."

The connection between transit access and sidewalk access is critical, but it is often overlooked. Too often we hear from transit providers that the sidewalks adjacent to their stops are the responsibility of the local city or county. The city and county planners aren't necessarily thinking about prioritizing improvements around transit stops that are managed by a separate agency or separate government entity.

Even where sidewalks exist, if they're cracked and crumbling, or too narrow or steep, they can be unusable for people with disabilities. Tanisha Sepúlveda, who was introduced in chapter 1, is a powerchair user who lives in Seattle and relies on the bus and light-rail when her partner cannot drive her. The sidewalk between her apartment complex and the closest bus stop has sections that are cracked with tree roots or filled with loose gravel from driveways, and many intersections are missing curb ramps. So, Sepúlveda rolls along the side of the street.

"I'll have people yell at me, then tell me to get out of the road, sometimes with profanity," Sepúlveda shared. "I understand that it does not look safe to them, and it is not safe, but it is even less safe for me to be on the sidewalk when the curb cuts are not in place, or there are dips in the cement, or roots have lifted up the sidewalk, or gravel."

Seattle has a dismal state of sidewalk repair. A 2017 audit found almost half of Seattle sidewalks inaccessible because of unrepaired cracks and bumps.[3] As in most jurisdictions in the US, private property owners are responsible for maintaining the sidewalk of their adjacent property, but these repairs can be expensive, and the city does not ensure that property owners fix dangerous or inaccessible conditions.

When curb ramps are missing, people using wheelchairs, walkers, or strollers have to find an adjacent driveway entrance and roll through traffic until they can get back on the sidewalk again. If a car has pulled forward into the intersection and blocked the curb ramp, trying to weave through drivers that have edged their way into a crossing can feel particularly dangerous to wheelchair users who may sit below the sightline of the driver, especially of larger SUVs or trucks.

Sometimes curb ramps have slopes that are too steep or large lips and cracks. Monteros explains: "Where the curb cut ends, and where the street starts, a lot of times that's broken up, or there's a crease right there. So, you really have to concentrate to make sure you don't fall forward. The only way we're actually going to be 'safe' is if everything is completely smooth and flat."

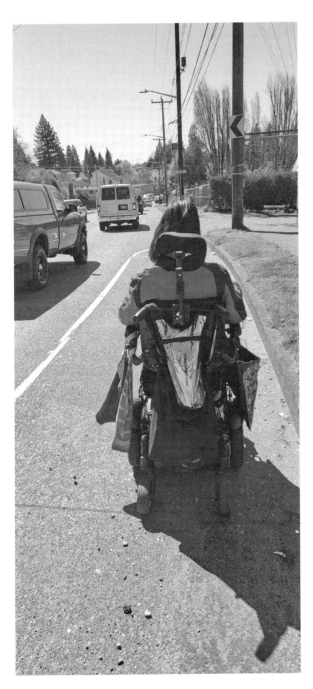

Figure 2-1: Tanisha Sepúlveda rolls along the street near her home where the sidewalk is inaccessible.

Image Description: The view is from behind as a woman with black hair in a power wheelchair rolls down the shoulder of a suburban-looking street next to a sidewalk.

Beyond more permanent barriers like missing or inadequate sidewalks or curb ramps, there are many transitory barriers that exist in the pedestrian right-of-way, such as overgrown plants and slippery leaves. In colder climates, ice and snow that isn't cleared properly can trap many people who are disabled inside for days, if not weeks.

"People often ask me how did I manage to get around in the weather lately with the snow and I tell them, I didn't. I didn't leave my house for eight days at one point," shares Seattle powerchair user Conrad Reynoldson.[4]

Mitchell Chong is a wheelchair user who grew up in Los Angeles and now lives in Lacey, a rapidly growing community near the large Joint Base Lewis-McChord military base in Washington State. Chong, who was born without arms or legs, relies on a powerchair for mobility. Cracked, blocked, or missing sidewalks are significant barriers to his access. Until he knows an area by heart, it's impossible for him to know whether he'll be able to get to a bus stop or other destination. "You can't take the same route that the GPS gives you," Chong explains.

The reality is that many local jurisdictions, states, and even our federal government have no assessment of where sidewalks exist and, if they do exist, their condition or accessibility. Compared to the extensive surveying and mapping of our road network, you have no way of knowing if a route is accessible for you to roll or walk along until you go out and try it. This is especially problematic for disabled people walking or rolling.

This gap in data is particularly frustrating because the Americans with Disabilities Act (ADA), which became law in 1991, required jurisdictions to create ADA transition plans within a year. These plans were to include an inventory of public facilities and public right-of-ways, and a schedule for remedying any issues. Dr.

Yochai Eisenberg at the University of Illinois at Chicago, in a national analysis conducted in 2020, found that only 13 percent of jurisdictions completed ADA transition plans, with many plans lacking the minimum requirements.[5]

While disabled people or organizations that represent disabled people can sue over the lack of accessibility in a community (and that often is the only way to convince a jurisdiction to make needed updates to curb ramps or sidewalks), the ADA does not permit people to sue over the lack of a plan.[6] Also, what is considered an ADA violation can be very limited. While the Department of Justice publishes an ADA toolkit to guide assessment and compliance with the ADA, that toolkit is primarily focused on the issue of curb ramps in the public right-of-way.[7] In 2011, the US Access Board proposed an updated set of Public Right-of-Way Accessibility Guidelines (commonly referred to by their acronym, PROWAG). These guidelines contain much more information about other accessibility needs, for example, accessible pedestrian signals for pedestrians who are blind and deaf. These updated and more comprehensive guidelines were finally finalized and published to the Federal Register in August 2023 and will become enforceable once adopted by the Department of Transportation and the Department of Justice.[8]

In the meantime, inaccessible sidewalks mean that people walking and rolling end up in the street with vehicles, a contributing factor in the road safety crisis. Nearly eight thousand pedestrians were killed in car crashes in the US in 2022, and an increasing percentage of people killed were Black and Latino.[9] Research from the University of Central Florida and the Florida DOT in 2022 reveals that the absence of a sidewalk "is one of the main factors that have significant impact on the expected number of pedestrian crashes at a specific location."[10]

Nondrivers Need Safe and Accessible Street Crossings

"I've waited for crosswalks for up to an hour because it's too difficult to know when to cross, explained Greg Hamby, a blind resident of the small sawmill and logging community of Longview, Washington.[11] For pedestrians who are blind or deafblind, crossings without audible and tactile signals called "accessible pedestrian signals," or APS for short, can be difficult or impossible to navigate safely. Especially on one-way streets or streets where there is infrequent and high-speed traffic, it can be impossible to distinguish when the drivers have a red light and it's safe to cross. Roundabouts are similarly challenging because traffic flows continually. Crossing requires trusting that drivers will see you and choose to yield.[12]

While many cities install APS when they put in new signals, there is a massive backlog of replacing inaccessible traffic signals in most American cities. Often this backlog is addressed only when disability advocates bring lawsuits to force cities to dedicate more resources to these updates. Before advocates sued, only 5 percent of New York City's signals included APS. In the 2021 settlement agreement, the city is required to install ten thousand accessible pedestrian signals over the next ten years.[13] Chicago had an even lower rate of accessible intersections—in 2023, only 1 percent of the city's intersections included APS, leading to a federal court ruling in 2023 that found that the failure to install APS constituted discrimination toward blind and low-vision pedestrians.[14]

Inadequate crossing time is also a safety concern and major stress point. While nondisabled adults walking quickly may be able to cross at a rate of four and a half feet per second, a child or someone with a walker crosses at a speed closer to one and a half to two feet per second, so if the crossing time is too short, they won't make it across before the light changes.[15]

Intersection spacing most often prioritizes the speedy movement of cars over the needs of people outside of vehicles. Jessie Singer, author of *There Are No Accidents: The Deadly Rise of Injury and Disaster—Who Profits and Who Pays the Price*,[16] explains, "We've built our cities and our suburbs and the road systems in between for speed, and in doing so, we have disregarded the potential of a vehicle ever interacting with a human body. When traffic engineers and government officials talk about speed, what they are really talking about is efficiency. And when they talk about efficiency, we always need to be asking: Efficiency for whom? The unspoken answer is always: Efficiency for vehicles and vehicles alone."

Todd Litman from the Victoria Transport Policy Institute explains that this experience has a technical name: "Every time you expand a road, or increase traffic speeds and traffic volumes, you're creating what's called the 'barrier effect.' Transportation engineers measure congestion delay to motorists, and frame it as the primary transportation problem, but do not measure barrier effect delay to nondrivers and don't consider it a problem."[17]

The federal standards that traffic engineers follow, published in the *Manual on Uniform Traffic Control Devices* (MUTCD), require that a minimum count of pedestrians be observed trying to cross an unsignalized intersection for a pedestrian signal to be installed.[18] Undoubtedly, there are many unsignalized crossings where people want to be able to cross but because of unsafe or inaccessible conditions choose not to, keeping the counts below where signals can be installed.

When pedestrians are faced with a five- or ten- or even fifteen-minute detour to get to the nearest crossing, crossing without a signal (pejoratively branded as jaywalking) may be a rational option. For pedestrians with mobility, sensory, or other disabilities, the longer detour may be the only option to cross with a curb ramp or accessible pedestrian signal. More often they are further disincentivized to take the trip at all.

In Seattle, what would be a ten-minute walk for someone who can step over a curb ramp could require thirty minutes of detours to find street corners with ramps. Powerchair user Erin Musser shared, "When you're trying to go three blocks down the street on your side of the street, sometimes you have to go a nine-block radius to get to where you're going."[19]

This becomes an even more pronounced issue when one side of a sidewalk is closed for construction, and pedestrians may be asked to cross the street more than once. This could be avoided if construction or demolition crews installed scaffolding. Despite ADA requirements for construction sites, temporary ramps aren't installed or detour paths aren't wide enough.

Widely spaced, unsafe, and inaccessible crossings are too often found on transit routes, which often run on larger arterials. The high speed of vehicles along these arterials, combined with long distances between crossings, can mean that transit stops get placed where there isn't a safe place to cross. I've heard from disabled transit riders who have to get off at bus stops farther away from their home because that's where there is an accessible crossing.

The challenges to pedestrian access become even greater when high-capacity bus routes or light-rail routes are constructed along freeway right-of-ways, and pedestrians are expected to cross highway on- and off-ramps, or feeder roads, to access transit stops. In the Seattle region, light-rail expansion is largely being built along freeway right-of-ways, meaning that people trying to access the system must cross where drivers are least expecting to encounter pedestrians. It is often an easier political lift and less costly to build rail along existing highway right-of-ways, and it may make sense to run bus rapid transit lines down major arterials where crossings

Figure 2-2: Construction closure of a sidewalk blocks a group of pedestrians in Seattle from being able to get up on the sidewalk or access the button to request a walk signal.

Image Description: A group of people, some using wheelchairs or white canes, cross the street and approach a sidewalk that is mostly blocked with temporary construction fencing and signage.

are less frequent and the buses can cover longer distances more quickly. But when these choices are made, investments must also be made to allow pedestrians—in particular pedestrians with disabilities, with children, with groceries—to cross these busy roads safely to access stops.

Even if a busy corridor has sidewalks, bike lanes, curb ramps, and accessible signals, that doesn't guarantee that it will be a comfortable or safe place for people waiting for the bus or people spending hours each day walking, rolling, or biking. Public health research is starting to show alarming connections between traffic noise exposure and health outcomes. A 2024 Transportation Research Board workshop will focus on this issue: "Active travelers' exposure to traffic noise is an important (but often overlooked) aspect of a supportive environment, due to the role of noise as not just an environmental hazard but also a mediator or proxy of safety, comfort, emissions, and air quality."[20] Modern vehicle design blocks out most of this road noise, but those of us who are outside of vehicles aren't so lucky.

Nondrivers Use Whatever Transit Is Available

Abby Griffith, who was born in Ethiopia, lost her eyesight as a child due to an eye infection. She was adopted at the age of fourteen by a teacher who lived on a farm in Ridgefield, Washington, about forty-five minutes north of Portland, Oregon.

Griffith remembers when she arrived in the US, she thought everyone speaking English sounded like birds. But she quickly learned English and also Braille. After high school, she started attending community college, but she struggled living in Ridgefield, where she had to rely on her mom for rides. "When I lived in Ridgefield, Washington, my siblings are all younger than me and my mom is a single mom," Griffith shared. "She was the only

Figure 2-3: During a walk/roll audit, a group crosses an unsignalized off-ramp of the I-90 freeway in Seattle, adjacent to the Judkins Park light-rail station. (Photo by David Seater)

Image Description: People wearing rain gear and holding umbrellas trying to block traffic so that other people, using white canes and wheelchairs, can get across a highway off-ramp.

person in the house who drove, and she is also a full-time worker, so it was not always easy for my mom to give everybody rides. There are so many different things I wanted to get involved with, but because I didn't have access to transportation and I didn't have a ride, I just sat there and just felt sad about it."

Griffith knew she needed to live somewhere with better transportation access so she wouldn't feel so trapped at home, lonely, and depressed. She secured a low-income rental apartment near a bus stop on the outskirts of Vancouver, Washington, approximately a twenty-minute drive from Ridgefield.

"When I graduated from high school, I made the decision to move out. The room I rented was right next to the bus number 30. It was life-changing for me to know that I have access to places. To get on the number 30 and go to college, go grocery shopping, or if I have events, social get togethers. I was the happiest. I was just so happy," Griffith shared. It still took her between two and three hours to get to her classes, because of the bus transfers, but she could get herself there when she needed to.

According to the Washington nondriver study, many nondrivers "felt they 'do not have transit options' citing 'lengthy and cumbersome' bus rides, difficult to understand schedules, and a lack of any public transit in some places as barriers to using transit."[21]

This study noted that the most prevalent concern of nondrivers is trip planning. Nondrivers with disabilities are often forced to patch together transit options to determine the least time intensive, least dangerous, or most physically possible way to get somewhere. It takes time—sometimes hours—to do this research before a trip, as I described in the opening of this chapter. While it's not often calculated into the time it takes to ride transit, this route planning time is often significant, especially when we want to go to a new destination.

Figure 2-4: Abby Griffith riding the bus from Vancouver to Portland.

Image Description: A Black woman wearing sunglasses and holding a white cane sits on a bus.

Many transit agencies employ travel trainers to teach people to travel plan and help them to feel comfortable using fixed route buses. A travel trainer will meet someone at their home and help them plan a comfortable route to work, the grocery store, or other locations they travel to frequently. While learning these skills can be life-changing, there are very often insurmountable barriers to mobility that are beyond what a transit agency is equipped to address, like roads without sidewalks or accessible places to cross. In some transit systems, the stations predate the ADA requirements and don't have elevators. Older transit vehicles are often inaccessible to people using wheelchairs or those with mobility disabilities. (In the 1980s, wheelchair users in Denver blocked buses to protest that they didn't have wheelchair lifts. This protest jump-started disability organizing and contributed to the advocacy that led to the passage of the ADA.[22])

For people who are disabled and cannot use fixed-route transit, public transit agencies are required to provide an accessible origin-to-destination alternative, in areas and during times where fixed-route service exists. Paratransit generally offers pickups within three-quarters of a mile from fixed-route transit stops and is required to pick up on the same days and for the same hours as fixed-route service. The number of trips someone requests cannot be limited, and they should be able to request service up to the day before.

Teaera Turner, who was introduced in chapter 1, lost her vision as an adult due to diabetes. She uses King County Metro paratransit, but its limitations can be frustrating. It's been difficult for her to get used to the paratransit "window" where appointment drop-offs can occur up to half an hour early and pickups can only be scheduled within an hour of the requested time. "I got here

Figure 2-5: Teaera Turner getting on a paratransit vehicle to go home at the end of her workday.

Image Description: A Black woman holding a white cane and smiling stands at the entrance to a paratransit vehicle.

thirty minutes early," Turner grumbled when she met me for coffee. "That's a lot of time."

Turner also expressed frustration with how difficult it can be for
the drivers to find her, resulting in her missing rides and getting
penalized by the system. This is exacerbated by the fact she can't
communicate with the driver directly. She has to call the central
dispatch system, who then communicates with the driver about
her whereabouts. Other paratransit users I've interviewed have
highlighted that a lack of driver training, or patience and understanding about how to work with people with different kinds of
disabilities and access needs, can result in unsafe or uncomfortable
situations.

When riders need to transfer between one paratransit service
area and another, for example to get from where they live to access
medical services in another county, the trips can be even more
difficult to coordinate. Some agencies in the greater Seattle region require three days' advance notice to provide rides to someone traveling from a neighboring transit agency, which can make
scheduling social activities or other travel even more burdensome.
It can be even more difficult to travel between jurisdictions outside
of peak hours. An orientation and mobility trainer I know spent
an afternoon searching for a twenty-four-hour fast-food establish-
ment, hospital, hotel lobby, or other location that was open and
safe at ten o'clock at night for one of his blind clients to wait as she
transferred between paratransit providers on her nightly commute
home from work. The transit agencies had arranged for the transfer to be at a park and ride lot, but the client felt unsafe waiting
at night in the dark without anyone else around. Unable to find
an open business nearby for her to wait, the trainer was able to
convince the transit agencies to switch the transfer point to a bus
station with more people around and better lighting.

Even for those who can't use fixed-route transit like buses or trains, qualifying for paratransit service can be a challenge. While it may be more obvious that someone with a visible physical disability may be unable to get to a bus stop, transit agencies may have a more difficult time evaluating how invisible disabilities, including cognitive disabilities, may impact the ability of someone to access fixed-route transit. Because of the high cost per ride of paratransit, services may be denied to people the provider feels could use fixed-route transit, especially people they perceive as younger and nondisabled. Sarah Carrillo, a recent graduate of Cornell University's master's program in urban planning, lives in New York City and has arthritis flare-ups that make using the stairs in the subway system difficult. But when she tried to qualify for paratransit service, she was denied.

Many people who would like to qualify for paratransit live outside the boundaries of service. Bridget Powell was struggling to afford the cost of living in Longview, Washington, so she moved back in with her parents who live farther out of town, outside the paratransit coverage area. "You have to be within two miles of the nearest city bus stop to be picked up by the Community Action Plan bus. I am five miles away," Powell explained. "I don't even have the option of walking because there are no sidewalks and it's not safe."

Recognizing there are many nondrivers who live outside of paratransit and transit service areas, or who have disabilities that require additional assistance getting to and from the pickup vehicles, the federal government funds "human services" transportation providers.[23] These providers can be everything from a senior center community shuttle, to a volunteer driver program in a rural area, to medical transport providers that receive reimbursements through Medicaid to take people to and from appointments. For many seniors who have aged out of driving, receiving services through one of these programs may be preferable to taking the bus, even if they do live within a service area, and for others, having "hand-to-hand" assistance getting from home to an appointment is necessary and not something that paratransit can provide.

Staci Sahoo, transportation director for social services agency Hopelink Mobility, which provides human transportation services throughout the Puget Sound region, explains, "There's still a wide gamut of people outside that window that can't be served through traditional paratransit, or it doesn't exist in their community. So, you have something like a volunteer driver program that's 'hand to hand,' that can take somebody, sit with them at their doctor's appointment, and make sure they get home safely. Paratransit just can't offer that level of service. And so, they're filling those little niche gaps."

But many of these "human services" transportation programs have limitations, sometimes geographic, sometimes in the type of assistance they can offer, or they are limited by trip purpose, for instance, they can only provide medical appointment transportation. Many people I interviewed recalled feeling judged or being denied trips for things that the providers deemed weren't essential or were outside the narrow funding restrictions of a particular program—like getting to a hairdressing appointment or stopping by a grocery store on the way back from a medical appointment.

Nondrivers Rely on Intercity Buses and Trains

Getting between communities, whether those are large regional centers or smaller rural towns, can be particularly challenging if you can't drive. In 2020 Smart Growth America noted that one million rural households do not have access to a car and emphasized the importance of ensuring these households have some form of transit access.[24] In previous generations, intercity bus routes provided some connectivity between more rural communities and larger regional population centers. But in the last decade, many of these routes have been eliminated. According to a 2021 National Geographic article on Greyhound service in the US, ten million people lack access to intercity bus travel.[25]

In the US, the lack of rural transportation options can limit access to medical care, including abortions. The *Seattle Times* shared a story of someone spending $1,200 on a cab ride to leave the state of Idaho and access abortion care in Oregon.[26] That extraordinarily high cost will undoubtedly be a barrier for many, and while networks of advocates and health care providers are working to provide transportation or reimburse transportation costs for people who need to seek abortions out of state, there will undoubtedly be people who aren't able to access these resources. There are many other reasons that people without access to driving might need to leave rural areas or small towns. To address the epidemic of missing and murdered women, First Nation communities in Canada and Native American communities in the US have called for better rural transit to provide options other than hitchhiking or walking along rural highways for community members who need to get places.[27]

Because of our limited Amtrak and Greyhound service, I've found myself flying to regional airports when the distances traveled could be easily made by bus or rail if those routes existed. I'm fortunate to have this option—for people traveling with wheelchairs, flying can be incredibly difficult and often results in damage to their wheelchairs or powerchairs, damages that can take months to repair or require a total replacement.

The lack of transportation in most rural areas also limits the ability of nondrivers to access parks and outdoor recreation activities.

A.P. is blind and lives in Seattle. She loves to ski and participate in other outdoor activities and reached out to me in frustration when she couldn't figure out any public transit options that would get her to a nearby rural community with a cross-country ski trail network. She gave up when she realized her only option was to pay close to $700 for ride hail each way.

"Outdoor recreation has long been a cultural cornerstone for a lot of Americans, and in the last decade or so we've begun to learn from experts that time outdoors and in green spaces has profound benefits for our bodies, minds, and souls," explains Kim Huntress Inskeep. Huntress Inskeep is a nondriver who worked with me at Disability Rights Washington to create our storymap, and she has gone on to launch Transit Trekker, a project aimed at helping people get to outdoor recreation trips using transit.

Accessing outdoor space, much of it located in more rural parts of the country, "is often an LSAT-worthy exercise," Huntress Inskeep says, because of the effort required to piece together local and regional transit schedules and figure out what roads or routes would be safe to walk or bike to get between transit options and the park entrances. She is advocating for greatly expanded rural transit options because they would not only provide rural nondrivers more connectivity but would allow people from other places to enjoy access to the outdoors regardless of whether they have the privilege to be able to drive themselves there.

Nondrivers Bike, Ride, and Roll

Ivy Take grew up in New Brunswick, Canada, and was born with nystagmus like me. Growing up, she knew that she didn't have enough vision to drive: "I wouldn't see things soon enough to make a safe decision, like to stop if something was crossing the road unexpectedly," she explained.

Take met her husband at the University of New Brunswick and started raising a family in Alberta. When her oldest child was in kindergarten, they made the move to Oro Valley, a suburb on the outskirts of Tucson, Arizona, for her husband's job. She made sure they found a house within walking distance of an elementary school, but the house wasn't within walking distance of anything else, and transit service in Oro Valley didn't exist at that time.

At first, Take was mostly reliant on her husband for rides, but he traveled a lot for work and so she was stuck at home too often. Then she saw her neighbor's golf cart, and after carefully mapping out routes she could take to avoid major arterials where she wouldn't be able to safely drive it, Take bought one herself. Next, she got seat belts installed for her elementary school–aged kids and strapped a large Rubbermaid container to the rear-facing seat to carry groceries.

The golf cart was a hit. Her kids' friends always wanted to get a ride with her because the prospect of getting somewhere in a golf cart was far more exciting than the usual ride in a minivan. "Boy, did it ever help me," Take said. "Just to get the kids to playdates, drive them to piano lessons. I could drive my son to Boy Scouts."

To cross larger streets, Take would often have to pull up on the sidewalk and push the pedestrian crosswalk button. She would frequently get stopped by the police, and she remembers being pulled over on her very first trip out of the neighborhood when she drove onto the sidewalk to push the walk button. Each time, she was able to explain her situation to the police and she was never ticketed, but in the back of her mind, Take always worried that she would get in trouble because of the legal uncertainty around her driving a golf cart on city streets.

Initially, Take even tried to get a license plate for her golf cart, but the department of licensing required proof of insurance, and the insurance company required a driver's license. The insurance company offered to issue the policy to her husband, but Take figured if she was driving the golf cart, it wouldn't cover her. So, she decided to risk driving without plates, which was what most golf cart users in Tucson do anyway.

As e-bikes became more widely available and affordable, Take replaced her golf cart with an e-bike. The e-bike batteries last far longer than the golf cart batteries, and she appreciates being able to ride longer distances. On a bike, she doesn't have to spend as much time plotting and mapping which roads she can ride on and how to get to a destination. It also helps that the Tucson region has continued to build out an extensive trail network, called "The Loop," which allows her to get more places using multiuse trails.

Many disabled people who cannot drive rely on bikes, trikes, e-bikes, and e-scooters for transportation. Like Take, I bike for transportation, and I've met lots of other low-vision adults who use bikes because they can't drive. While it is not safe for someone like Take or me, with less than 20/40 vision, to drive a multi-ton vehicle at 75 miles per hour, we can safely pilot a small, light vehicle going less than 20 miles per hour. People who can't drive because of physical or cognitive disabilities may find biking works for them too, and I've gotten to know people with autism as well as those with mental health conditions who find biking is a safe option when driving is not.

Cody Shane Fairweather lives in the small rural community of Chewelah, Washington, in a farm valley near the border with Canada. Because of developmental disabilities, Fairweather can't drive, but he rides a three-wheeled bike (like an adult-sized trike) to get around town, from his house to the library, to the grocery store. "It gets me where I have to go," he explained, showing off his trike with a large back cargo basket. "The basket helps me haul groceries and books and stuff."

As in many rural communities, the main street of Chewelah also serves as Highway 395, connecting the regional center of Spokane to a busy agricultural border crossing with Canada. There are no bike lanes on this road, and the city council passed an ordinance banning people from riding bikes on the sidewalk.

"It's really not a bike-friendly town," Fairweather commented. "There's no bike lanes. We're not allowed to ride on the sidewalks on Main Street—we have to push our bicycles. It's kind of a pain." Crossing this state highway is also a challenge. There's only one stoplight in town, which Fairweather has to detour out of his way to use to get from his home to his job at the library. Traffic volumes are only expected to get worse as the state invests in a major highway widening project along a section of this highway closer to Spokane.

For people who use trikes, recumbents, handcycles, and cargo e-bikes, where bike infrastructure exists, it often isn't accessible. Bollards used to keep cars out of bike lanes can be too narrow for wider bike frames; bike parking often can't accommodate these "nontraditional" bikes, and they can be too heavy to carry up and down stairs and too large to fit in elevators. Trikes, recumbents, and handcycles are also expensive, making them increased targets for theft.

Leroy Moore is a Black disabled cyclist who has competed in the Paralympics. He got around on a three-wheeled bike when he was living in the East Bay near San Francisco. Moore described frequently getting pulled over by police who would tell him either that it's unsafe to ride in the street or that he should not ride on the sidewalk and should ride on the street.[28] Although bikes are allowed on Bay Area Regional Transit (BART), it is often impossible to bring heavier cargo bikes, trikes, or recumbents on transit. Moore has had two trikes stolen when he locked them at Oakland BART stations.

While the increased availability of e-bikes and e-trikes, including less-expensive models, is creating more opportunities for some disabled people to get where they need to go, wheelchair users have few affordable options because of the expense and difficulty in sourcing powerchairs that are designed to meet their needs.

Ian Mackay is a powerchair user who was a mountain biker before he became paralyzed. Being outdoors has always been important to his mental health, and so after his injury he spent a lot of time getting the equipment he needs to do long powerchair rides outdoors. He started a nonprofit, Ian's Ride, that supports other disabled people by giving them opportunities to experience the outdoors. Annually, he organizes a three-day "Sea to Sound" supported tour along a rail-to-trail segment on the Olympic Peninsula in Washington State. Mackay also organizes annual challenge rides for which he pushes equipment manufacturers to provide powerchairs, nudging them to advance their technology to support traveling longer distances in more weather conditions over different types of terrain. In 2022, Mackay rode the Great American Rail-Trail from Washington, DC, to Columbus, Ohio, around 450 miles. In previous years, he's ridden across Washington State, over the Cascade Range.

"Oftentimes, people's lifestyles are shaped by the equipment that they have," Mackay explained in frustration. "People could do so much more, and the equipment is determining the direction of their life. A family should be able to go spend the day at Disneyland and not run out of batteries."

Figure 2-6: Mackay and a group of participants in the annual Sea to Sound ride he organizes with his nonprofit Ian's Ride. (Photo by Jesse Major)

Image Description: A White man in a powerchair with waist-length dreadlocks rolls on a paved path in the woods. Behind him are other people rolling with different kinds of power and manual wheelchairs and bicycles.

Powerchairs usually run on lead-acid batteries that have a very limited range and have to be replaced annually. With the lead-acid batteries that came with his chair, Mackay has a range of about fourteen miles. In contrast, the lithium battery pack he put together to use on his chair gets closer to eighty miles. But lithium batteries are more expensive than the lead-acid batteries, so insurance often won't cover them. Because most people rely on insurance to cover the cost of their chairs, wheelchair manufacturers are motivated to build what insurance will approve, not necessarily what wheelchair users need or want.

As much as those of us who can bike, e-bike, trike, or roll will benefit from accessible and continuous infrastructure for biking and rolling, it's important to recognize that this same infrastructure, especially if designed without consideration, can create barriers for other disabled people. If you are a person who has a mobility disability or chronic health condition that makes walking or rolling difficult, and you rely on driving or being driven to get places, having parking access close to where you need to be, parking access with wheelchair loading that is not obstructed by or in conflict with a bike lane, is critical.

"Sometimes there's an assumption that if a project improves active transportation safety overall, then it's a win for disabled people. That is not always the case," explains Maddy Ruvolo, who is a disabled transportation planner for San Francisco Municipal Transportation Agency and a member of the United States Access Board. Ruvolo points out how protected cycling lanes can make it impossible for people with wheelchairs or mobility aids to safely exit a car and get to the sidewalk.

"In my experience, there is often a design solution that maintains or increases access for disabled people while improving safety for cyclists," she elaborated, explaining that parking-protected cycling lanes can and should be designed with enough space for someone to safely get out of a vehicle with an accessible path of travel from the parking to the curb. "The key thing is that access doesn't happen automatically: accessibility has to be baked into the design process," Ruvolo offers as a reminder to planners and cycling infrastructure advocates.

For people who are blind or low vision, feeling comfortable navigating often comes from being familiar with a space and knowing what to anticipate, and so encountering unexpected barriers can be disorienting and dangerous. Too often, "quick-build," pop-up, or temporary street redesigns, intended to minimize community opposition to change because they are only experiments and not permanent changes, are not designed with accessibility in the forefront. The consequence of this is that blind and low-vision or other disabled community members suddenly find that a street they knew how to navigate safely has become unnavigable because of new bike infrastructure, pedestrian plazas, or floating bus stops.

Because many of these new streetscape designs are being tried in communities for the first time, there is little standardization, so a person who is blind trying to understand if a tactile strip indicates they are ending a road or crossing into a shared bike lane or floating bus stop doesn't have an answer. Inconsistencies between treatments can be dangerous: a low-vision power wheelchair user I know flipped her chair off a curb when she thought she was rolling down a curb ramp marked by the bright yellow tactile strip. But instead, the yellow strip was demarcating a bus stop in a transit center.

"Accessibility is not a competition but rather a collaboration. It involves problem-solving and focuses on the goal of leaving no one behind," shared Vancouver, British Columbia–based disabled writer and policy analyst Gabrielle Peters.[29] "Where prioritization must occur, it must be focused on those with the least access currently, those facing the most barriers, and this includes considering the impact of any and all intersecting oppression, such as racism, gender discrimination, income, and classism."[30]

Nondrivers Ask or Pay for Rides

When you're a nondriver, having a community of friends, parents, spouses, children, or neighbors you can rely on to give you rides can make the difference between being able to participate in activities outside your home or not. Disabled adults (age 18–64) travel as passengers in vehicles for a greater share of trips than nondisabled adults, according to the Bureau of Transportation Statistics.[31]

But too often, we overlook the emotional burden of relying on social connections to get places. The nondriver study in Washington State found that women, younger people, lower-income people, and disabled nondrivers were more likely to feel that their transportation needs were a burden on others.[32] This unease and strain on relationships unquestionably impacts how often those of us who can't drive feel comfortable asking for rides. Having an option to travel without asking for a favor is often important for our mental health, and sometimes it is even key to our safety and physical well-being.

Amanda Sutherland, who is legally blind, shared: "Whenever I call or text somebody asking for a ride I start to wonder, are they going to get back to me or not? Should I call a second person? There are times I would rather walk, even several miles, than deal with the anxiety of finding a ride."

When nondrivers feel like we can't ask for another favor, or we simply don't have a person in our lives we can turn to, often our only other option is to pay, calling a taxi or summoning ride hail.

In 2014, before the arrival of Uber, when I traveled for work around the US, if a client couldn't pick me up at the airport, I was usually stuck. I remember waiting for over an hour for a cab at the airport in Springfield, Missouri. And then, within a year, Uber and Lyft were everywhere, and getting to places outside of New York City got much easier for me. Because of venture capital subsidies, ride hail was initially very affordable. Once, I missed my train back to New York from Hartford, Connecticut, and got a three-hour Uber ride for not much more than I would have paid for an Amtrak ticket.

But even when rides were more heavily subsidized, ride hail remained too expensive for many disabled nondrivers to use with any regularity. People who are disabled, regardless of education level attained, are much less likely to be employed.[33] According to the Center for American Progress, disabled adults are twice as likely to experience poverty than their nondisabled peers.[34] And if you need a wheelchair-accessible vehicle, you are out of luck. The ADA doesn't have the same wheelchair accessibility requirements for for-hire vehicles as it has for public transit.[35]

Some jurisdictions have tried to mandate and fund an increase in wheelchair-accessible taxicabs. For instance, in 2013, disability advocates in New York City won a legal settlement to dramatically increase the number of accessible taxicabs, funded through a thirty-cent surcharge on for-hire rides. The goal was to have half of the fleet wheelchair accessible in ten years. But as that deadline approaches, the number of accessible yellow cabs remains under 40 percent, and as of March 2022, only 69 of 1,418 green cabs that serve the outer boroughs were accessible.[36]

In Seattle, since 2014, ten cents of every dollar spent on a ride-hail trip has gone to support the purchase of wheelchair-accessible taxis for the county fleet.[37] But drivers claim there's not enough demand for wheelchair-accessible rides to make driving a wheelchair-accessible taxi worth the additional cost of the vehicle and higher fuel costs, so there's still a large discrepancy in wait times between wheelchair-accessible taxis and ride hail.[38]

Outside of major metropolitan areas, it can be almost impossible to find a wheelchair-accessible taxi. This means that, unless you can afford your own wheelchair-accessible van, you have to figure out how to get all of your transportation needs met using transit, paratransit, or the limited services offered by human services transportation providers, if one with wheelchair-accessible vehicles operates in your community.

People who use service animals also face barriers with ride hail. While it's illegal to refuse to give a ride to someone with a service animal, many users who are blind report that refusals are not uncommon.[39] For users who are blind or low vision, finding the right vehicle can also be a challenge. This is true for me, as I can't read license plates unless I'm bending down next to the vehicle, and I can't recognize vehicle brands. I've tried to get into cars that weren't my ride before, and at airports, I've often had drivers leave before I can identify them.

Taxis and ride hails are not always available in more rural areas, and availability fluctuates in many areas. During the pandemic, areas that once had reliable ride-hail service saw the drivers vanish as demand for rides decreased, leaving riders who still needed the services without options they had come to rely on. Grace Hope from Tacoma, Washington, who was introduced in chapter 1, explained: "When the pandemic happened, two things really knocked me sideways. Not having vaccination, I wasn't comfortable using public transportation. My backup transportation option was ride hail, and there just weren't any drivers available."

Relying on others to drive us places—whether that's a friend or an Uber driver—is only a stopgap measure to true transportation independence, the kind of transportation independence that is possible only if we are able to live in communities that are designed to reduce car dependency.

Nondrivers Move to Access Services (When We Can Afford To)

Micah Lusignan, who was introduced in chapter 1, lost his vision as a young teen and spent his childhood in Washington and Texas. After a few years at community college, he transferred to the University of Washington in Seattle and looked for housing near campus. But housing near the University District is expensive. Lusignan found a shared room for $700 a month, but even that was a stretch financially, and he found it stressful sharing a bedroom. To make ends meet, he tried to spend no more than seventy-five cents a meal. Even with these challenges, Lusignan loved living in a part of town with light-rail service, frequent buses, and many locations within walking distance. "My house was a three-minute walk from Trader Joe's, a seven-minute walk from Safeway, a ten-minute walk from Target, a five-minute walk from the YMCA. That was the first time I ever lived in a place where I actually felt like I could be fully independent in the sense of the way that I traveled," Lusignan recalled.

After he graduated, Lusignan decided he wanted his own room, which meant moving to a more affordable area. He found a room in a shared home in Lynnwood, a suburb to the north of Seattle. The nearest transit stop was more than a mile away from the house, with sections of missing sidewalk on the route. The nearest grocery store was an hour away on foot, in a suburban mall with a giant parking lot that is difficult to navigate. While there is a sidewalk the whole way, Lusignan ran into blackberry bushes that had overgrown the sidewalk. He often found himself stretching his budget to pay for a ride hail to get to the bus to take him into the city. He would much prefer to live closer in, but rent in Seattle is beyond his budget. To live where there is good transit service and a complete sidewalk network, "it's a privilege, or it's an immense sacrifice," Lusignan concluded.

Again and again, in interviews with nondrivers, I hear stories about the pressure of high housing prices pushing people outside transit access. As "walkability" has become a premium, the places with the best pedestrian accessibility are also the most expensive. People with disabilities who most rely on sidewalk connectivity often cannot afford to live where they have that access.

"More affordability means moving farther out. Moving farther out means more limited transportation," said Vaughn Brown, who is blind and hard of hearing. He struggled to afford rising rents outside of Portland, Oregon, so moved to Eastern Washington, where the cost of living is closer to what he is able to earn.

Since 1965, housing prices in the United States have risen 115 percent, while income has risen only 15 percent.[40] The disparity between home prices and incomes is even greater in cities that have experienced rapid job and population growth like Seattle, without a comparable increase in available housing. This disconnect is having profound consequences on younger people and families without generational wealth as buying into the housing market has become out of reach. Many nondrivers who need to live in places with reliable transit and complete sidewalk networks just can't. The most affordable rentals are along busy highways in the exurbs, or even out of the city entirely, in rural areas where transit may not exist.

I met Erica Jones, introduced in chapter 1, when she was living in Edmonds, about an hour north of Seattle in Snohomish County. Jones needed to go to frequent doctor's visits in Seattle, which required her to transfer from the bus service in Snohomish County to King County Metro bus service. Her trip would take at least an hour and a half each way, if all the schedules aligned. Often, they didn't, and at times, when traffic delayed the King County buses, Jones would arrive too late to make the transfer to the Snohomish County bus. This proved extremely difficult, as her power wheelchair doesn't fit into her friends' cars and wheelchair-accessible cabs are not reliably available. Once, the bus driver, recognizing that traffic delays made Jones miss the last connection, called in and got permission to drive her to her bus stop.

As the light-rail service area in Seattle expanded, Jones and her roommates started looking for housing closer to the city, and they felt incredibly fortunate to find an apartment near the soon-to-open light-rail station at Northgate. On the first day of train service at the new station, Jones was on the platform. Her enthusiasm for the new station and access to transportation was so evident that she was interviewed by a number of news outlets covering the station openings that day.

That kind of access to light-rail is the dream of many nondrivers I have interviewed. But for most, the costs of living within walking or rolling distance to light-rail are prohibitive.

Devin Silvernail works as a policy advisor to Seattle Councilmember Tammy Morales. Like me, he has nystagmus and is a nondriver and a parent (he was introduced earlier in the book when he talked about his experience of covering up why he cannot drive). Silvernail has spent years doing tenant organizing and working on housing affordability issues and was involved in organizing a successful campaign to win voter approval for a social housing initiative in Seattle.

"Housing is just one piece. Infrastructure for mobility is just one piece," Silvernail explains. "We really need to think about all

Figure 2-7: Erica Jones about to board a train at the Northgate light-rail station.

Image Description: A White woman smiles, sitting in a powerchair in front of a light-rail train.

of those things as an ecosystem." Having key services within close proximity is essential to living comfortably without driving, he explained. And those services need to be culturally relevant and affordable.

Silvernail recalled how after his toddler got sick, he had to spend over an hour on transit each way to get to a pharmacy that was open after 9:00 p.m. For a driver, it would have been a quick ten-minute trip, but for those of us without access to driving, not having a local pharmacy has significant costs.

These costs, and the hostility Silvernail encounters from drivers when navigating the city in his cargo bike with his kid, led him to question whether it's worth staying. His wife has French citizenship, so they've made the decision to move to France in 2024 to live in a small city where they can walk and bike everywhere, and where all their neighbors can too. "There's literally a grocery store below our apartment," Silvernail told me with great anticipation. As his daughter grows up, he also wants her to have the freedom to walk and bike places safely, and he knows that in Seattle, and in the rest of the United States, he just can't afford to live in a community where she could do that.

Nondrivers Stay Home

Because just about every trip takes longer, and may be costly, physically demanding, or dangerous, nondrivers tend to travel less. The 2023 study on the demographics of nondrivers commissioned by the Washington State legislature found that "at least once a week if not more often, 23 percent of nondrivers will skip going somewhere because of a problem with transportation, 22 percent will be late when not driving, 34 percent worry about being able to get somewhere, and 39 percent worry about inconveniencing friends and family." The survey found that accessing medical appointments was found to be the most difficult for nondrivers, with 35 percent of respondents saying that this was somewhat difficult, very difficult, or not possible.[41]

The Bureau of Transportation Statistics survey data shows that on average disabled people aged 18–64 make one fewer trip per day than people without disabilities (2.6 compared to 3.6 trips).[42] And travel times are longer for disabled nonworkers, even though trips are shorter. "Despite taking shorter trips, non-workers with disabilities have slightly longer travel times, traveling an average of 23.3 minutes per trip versus 21.0 minutes per trip for non-workers without disabilities." The disparity is even greater for work trips. "Workers with disabilities travel an average of 9.4 versus 12.0 miles for workers without disabilities."[43]

Among nondrivers, the Washington study found that low-income and female nondrivers are more likely to skip going somewhere more than once per week, compared to male nondrivers or those with incomes over $56,000 a year. Nondrivers who are female, lower-income, younger, and disabled reported worrying more about being able to get somewhere and about inconveniencing others more than their male, older, higher-income, and nondisabled peers.[44]

For nondriving parents, the added difficulty in making trips means that their children may also miss out. Kimberly Glass from Reno, who we met in chapter 1, described not being able to get her daughter, who has complex medical needs, to a specialist located outside the paratransit service area.

"As a parent, it's heart-wrenching because I can't really be a mom and do what's needed for her because I was born a certain way," Glass told me.

Most schools, clinics, and opportunities for kids assume a driving parent. This can turn parents (usually moms) who can drive into full-time chauffeurs. For parents who don't have time to drive, or for nondriving parents, it can limit the opportunities for their kids. Dr. Kelcie Ralph from Rutgers University published research on the impact of transportation access on the intergenerational transmission of economic standing. She found that "young adults who were Carless growing up did indeed complete less education than their matched peers who always had access to a car. They also worked for pay less often and earned less."[45]

Nondrivers Rely on Remote Access and Delivery Services

The acceptance of remote work, remote schooling, and the availability of online social activities accelerated during the pandemic, making it easier for nondrivers with internet access and some technological know-how to build connections. Remote work in particular benefits workers who are disabled, removing the burden of traveling to an office and having to navigate inaccessible office environments.

The Department of Labor analyzed employment and home internet data between 2019 and 2020 and found that disabled workers between the ages of 25 and 64 with internet at home were 20 percentage points more likely to retain employment than those without internet at home. Interestingly, for nondisabled workers, "there is no clear association between home internet subscriptions and employment retention."[46]

Increased delivery options through Amazon or meal and grocery delivery apps have made it easier to get household goods and food for nondrivers who can afford these services. Grace Hope relies on DoorDash to get medication and food deliveries so they don't have to pay for ride hail or try to carry heavy items, which is difficult for them. "I pay so many delivery services to get things to my house that I can't," they say. For shoppers who are blind, grocery delivery can mean not having to try to find a store employee available to help them navigate the store and find items. Many of the more affordable big-box stores tend to be located on the outskirts of urban areas, where there are fewer transit options, so ordering groceries or household supplies to be delivered from these stores may be the only option for nondrivers.

But having meals or groceries delivered may mean that a nondriver is missing an opportunity to make critical social connections or learn about other needed services. For instance, when a nondriver travels into town or to a community center to pick up food, they may learn about health care or mental health programs and build relationships with staff and other people at the community center.

Some people lack reliable internet or don't know how to use the technology, making online social connections difficult or impossible. Other nondrivers don't enjoy connecting remotely, so online activities, especially social activities, are no replacement for having transportation access.

Cody Shane Fairweather, who you may remember was born with developmental disabilities and lives in the small farming community of Chewelah, Washington, emphasized the importance of transportation access for well-being: "Without transportation, people with disabilities become isolated, and when we become isolated, we become depressed," he told me.

"Transportation matters a lot across the board for disabled people, and particularly for people who might have a lot of difficulty accessing common space more broadly, because if you don't have transit, you don't have the outside world, effectively," Noor Pervez from the Autistic Self Advocacy Network explains. Without transportation, disabled people who live with family or caregivers may lack access to outside legal or other support resources, resources that could help them get out of situations where they are facing abuse or not getting their needs met.

Pervez pointed out this is particularly important for people who may be living with and getting support from aging parents. As their parents age and can no longer meet all their care needs, it's critical they be connected to other community resources. "The relationships that you can build if you have the capacity to leave, even just for a little bit at a time, is a huge, huge deal."

Nondrivers Need Local Connections

Building connections in our community, beyond our homes, is essential. Access isn't only about creating transportation systems where we can get where we need to go without the harms and exclusions of car dependency, it's also about envisioning our public right-of-ways as public spaces where we can build community and connections.

In the summer of 2021, I got a permit from the City of Seattle to shut down the street in front of our house to through-traffic and host weekly block parties. By its third year, the weekly evening block party had become an institution. Now if the adults on the block, too tired from a long day at work, threaten to cancel one, we face a kid revolt.

I also depend more on my block community than perhaps many of my neighbors who can drive. I don't have the ability to jump in a car and go visit a friend across town in an easy fifteen minutes or head out of town to the woods or the mountains on the weekend. My block is really the heart of my social and recreational world and where I spend most of my time, and I believe that's something to aspire to.

Mobility justice theorist Mimi Sheller from Worcester Polytechnic Institute writes about the concept of the "kinetic elite" for

Figure 2-8: Our block party in the summer of 2023.

Image Description: A group of children of various ages play in a suburban street with bikes and scooters. Behind them, adults are gathered around tables set in the street as the sun begins to set.

whom constant travel is the signal of wealth, connections, and prestige. Sheller asks us to question our cultural idealization of travel for the sake of travel, the colonial fantasy of the exotic vacation or jet-setting digital nomad.[47]

And while perhaps less extreme than the jet-setting kinetic elite that Sheller writes about, in some ways the privilege of driving creates a kinetic elite of drivers in our local communities. There are the direct public health burdens that driving creates for those who live along busy roads, and there are also the other less obvious costs of driving. When it's easy for us to zoom across town, or out of town, this comes at the cost of our local connections, the time we spend with our neighbors and those we share close physical proximity to. As we face more climate extremes, it's these very local connections, these relationships with our neighbors, that will provide us the most support. With the inevitable future of more extreme weather events, it's these neighborhood connections that are the most critical to all our survival.[48]

CHAPTER 3

Nondrivers Need What Everyone Needs: Here's How We Get It

W HAT NONDRIVERS NEED—what we all need—is a transformation of the way we organize mobility, housing, and public space so that we have options for getting around that do not rely on driving a car. We need safe, connected places to walk, roll, and ride; transit that is as reliable as driving; and land use and remote access opportunities that reduce how much we have to travel. This transformation can move us away from the most harmful public health and climate impacts of automobility and start to create a more inclusive mobility system.

While it's much easier to imagine—and less disruptive to current entrenched systems—solutions that aid the mobility of nondrivers by providing drivers or vehicle access (such as autonomous vehicles), these stopgaps only further entrench us in car dependence. Instead, I challenge us to prioritize more difficult and larger-scale transformations. Some of these changes will take time, political capital, and a large shift in how we allocate resources. Ultimately, if we want our children to live in a world where car ownership and the ability to drive aren't determinants of their access to work, school, services, and community, we can't keep enabling the status quo.

Retrofitting our communities so we can live without car dependency is going to be a profoundly difficult task. It will only be possible if those of us not well served by the current system can organize and can build a big enough coalition to demand change. Just as we transformed our communities in the last hundred years to center and prioritize car movement, in the next hundred years we can, if we want to, build an entirely different future.

Make Nondrivers Visible

Nondrivers are often seen as an insignificant part of the population: too young, too old, too disabled. Not driving is often viewed as a transitory state—once someone earns enough money to afford a car, resolves a license suspension, or turns sixteen—they will return to the ranks of people with valid mobility needs. These beliefs lead to an erasure of nondrivers. One of the first steps in valuing the needs of nondrivers is counting how many people are truly not served by automobility. Because that total, even if our calculation methods are imperfect, can correct the falsehood that nondrivers are too rare, too insignificant a percentage of the population to bother to prioritize our needs.

In Washington, the 2023 nondriver study commissioned by the state legislature served this purpose. When I first started saying that a quarter of our state's population were nondrivers, based on a simple calculation of the number of driver's licenses compared to the total population, planners and policymakers were often incredulous. But having this figure backed up by more extensive analysis done by respected transportation consultants makes it more difficult to discount.

The Washington research referenced similar research from Wisconsin. In 2020, disability advocates there were able to convince Wisconsin's Department of Transportation (WisDOT) to form a Non-Driver Advisory Committee. One of the first tasks of this committee was to understand how many nondrivers there are and where they live. So, WisDOT conducted an analysis of driver's license holders, car registrations, and census data to create GIS data showing where nondrivers live throughout the state. In total, they estimated that 31 percent of their population are nondrivers.[1]

Denise Jess, one of the co-chairs of the Non-Driver Advisory Committee, is also the executive director of the Wisconsin Council of the Blind & Visually Impaired. She believes that 31 percent is likely as undercount, as they were unable to include undocumented nondrivers and people who have licenses but limit their driving or stopped driving because of safety concerns.

Using the data and maps produced by this research, the Non-Driver Advisory Committee has been able to push for greater visibility and consideration of nondrivers. Committee co-chair Tamara Jackson, policy analyst and legislative liaison for the Wisconsin Board for People with Developmental Disabilities, shared: "When you overlay where the transit is, where the routes are, and where the stops are with where people who are nondrivers actually live, those two things don't overlap." This forces transportation planners to consider whether people are unable to use transit because "it doesn't go where they need to go, or they can't get to it."

The Wisconsin Board for People with Developmental Disabilities and Wisconsin Council for the Blind collaborated with Disability Rights Wisconsin, the Centers for Independent Living, and the Greater Wisconsin Agency on Aging Resources to use the nondriver data to help inform lawmakers about the importance of funding transportation services for people without other options. In speaking to elected leaders from more rural areas, Jess said she will remind them that "some of those counties have 30 to 40 percent of the population that are nondrivers." In these conversations, the lawmakers frequently tell her that they have family members who can't drive. Jess reminds them that while they may be able to meet the mobility needs of their loved ones currently, that isn't true for every family, and that from a strictly financial standpoint, providing rural transit so someone can remain in their home and in their community is far less expensive than what it costs to institutionalize someone in an assisted living facility.

"There is a perception that nondrivers are people with disabilities or older adults, but I feel it's important to emphasize the large and growing population of low- and middle-income working people who are becoming nondrivers, many for economic reasons," explained Jackson. "Especially as car manufacturers are focusing on building higher-end models with correspondingly higher price points—rather than trying to sell more lower-priced cars—vehicles are becoming an asset many people cannot afford to own and maintain."

"This is a systems issue," Jess added. "There are a lot of us. It's important to know as a nondriver that you are not alone." Jackson agrees that having a concrete number has helped with their advocacy for better access. "No one can get away from that number—31 percent of the population being nondrivers. It's a shocking number for us in Wisconsin." Jackson encourages other states to conduct a similar analysis to understand what percentage of their state population are nondrivers: "I don't think that it's necessarily different in other states, at all," she suggests.

Create Safe, Connected Spaces to Walk, Roll, and Ride

In the early months of the coronavirus pandemic as stay-at-home orders transformed daily routines, many people who would normally get where they needed to go by driving found themselves walking around their neighborhoods for perhaps the first time. An April 2020 article from the *Seattle Times* featured an interview with a retired couple who began to notice how much of their community lacked sidewalks. "This neighborhood is not set up for walking. . . . Sidewalks would be a huge help, for starters. And crosswalks," Shoreline resident Garry Lingerfelt shared with the reporter.[2] It took Lingerfelt and his partner only a few weeks of navigating their community on foot to realize how it would be more comfortable to walk if they had a safe space to do so.

The "solution" to reducing car dependency isn't rocket science. I don't expect you to be surprised by the suggestions in the following sections, but as you read through the rest of this chapter, ask yourself why we haven't been able to invest in these changes and instead are so tantalized by the allure of new technological solutions (like autonomous vehicles or mobility as a service). What nondrivers need isn't groundbreaking, and it doesn't require new research or the development of new technology. What we need is the organizing power and the coalition-building skills to demand that we stop prioritizing the mobility of cars over the health and connectivity of our communities.

Slow the Movement of Vehicles and Improve Crossings

The most critical element of making streets safer and more comfortable for people walking, rolling, or riding is slowing the movement of vehicles. Many local jurisdictions are lowering speed limits to reduce the number and severity of crashes. Engineering choices that narrow lane width and force vehicles to travel slower with chicanes, raised crosswalks, or speed bumps also will result in safer and more comfortable spaces. Traffic diverters to create low-traffic neighborhood streets not only improve the environment on the streets but have been shown to reduce vehicle traffic overall.[3]

Slower roads with fewer and narrower lanes, more frequent crossings, and building entrances close to the street create a much more comfortable pedestrian environment than long blocks, multilane roads, and buildings set behind giant parking lots. Narrower streets with slower speeds also reduce traffic noise, the detrimental health effects of which we are just beginning to understand.

Crossings can also be made safer by prioritizing the comfortable movement of pedestrians over the speed that vehicles can get through an intersection. Every signalized crossing (a crossing with a stoplight) must be updated to include signals with audible and tactile feedback, and signals should be timed so that people who move more slowly still have time to cross.

In 2020, the City of Seattle agreed to slow its walk signal timing from three to three and a half feet per second to two and a half. They also agreed to designate some intersections with even slower crossing times where there is a high concentration of seniors or residents who are disabled (though this approach begs the question of how someone who needs extra time can cross safely when they travel outside of their immediate neighborhood).

Some newer models of accessible pedestrian signals include a feature where the user can press and hold for a longer walk signal. Another feature that is standard in Tokyo, and also deployed in Bellevue, Washington, is an audible signal that makes different sounds for north–south versus east–west crossings, allowing blind pedestrians to more easily orient themselves. But these both require that an audible pedestrian signal is installed in the first place, which isn't a guarantee in far too many communities.

Another way to increase the amount of time pedestrians have to cross, and to prevent pedestrians from being hit by turning vehicles, is to restrict the ability of vehicles to turn right through a red light while pedestrians have the walk signal. Only a few cities in

North America have this regulation (including New York City and Montreal) but other cities are exploring this possibility.

Assess Where Gaps Exist

"When we look at digital maps that we have in phones today, they're actually just representing the automobile network. When you press walking mode, they assume that you're a slow-moving car along the roadways that have that connected transportation layer. But we don't have that connected transportation layer for pedestrians," explained Dr. Anat Caspi, director of the OpenSidewalks project at the University of Washington's Taskar Center for Accessible Technology.

The OpenSidewalks project uses open data sources and machine learning, verified by on-the-ground community audits, to map sidewalk networks. Its data schema includes more detail about the pedestrian environment, data that aren't typically collected in ADA assessments, such as sidewalk slope, minimal effective width, and the lighting environment. And because the project is using open data sources, the data it collects is also open for public domain use, so anyone can input their travel needs and be able to generate the best route.[4]

By May 2023 OpenSidewalks had mapped eleven cities in six countries, including Los Angeles, California; São Paulo, Brazil; Quito, Ecuador; and Gran Valparaíso and Santiago, Chile. Dr. Caspi notes that each community may have different priorities for accessibility—while one community might be focused on curb ramps, another could prioritize barriers created by trees. For some cities, like Seattle, with steep hills, mapping publicly accessible elevators within buildings to traverse the elevation change between blocks is critical. In snowy climates like Minneapolis, elevated, enclosed pedestrian walkways between buildings are part of the pedestrian network.

OpenSidewalks began with an effort by Dr. Caspi to create an accessible pedestrian routing tool for Seattle, called AccessMap. Now available both on desktops and as an app, AccessMap allows users to find the best route to walk or roll using the data. Open-Sidewalks data can also be used by planners for calculating walk-sheds, for instance, comparing access from a bus stop for someone who uses a wheelchair to someone who doesn't.

In Washington, after the nondriver report was released in February 2023, the state legislature agreed to fund OpenSidewalks to complete a sidewalks data project so communities in Washington have a better assessment of where pedestrian connective investments are most needed, not just on state highways, but also county and city right-of-ways. The legislature allocated $5 million for the 2023–24 biennium, with a promise of an additional $5 million for the following biennium to complete a data analysis of the condition of the sidewalks along every road in the state. Ultimately, this data will help Washington State and local jurisdictions prioritize where sidewalk repairs and missing sidewalk construction are most necessary and will give advocates a tool for pushing local jurisdictions to secure the funding necessary to make these changes.

Dr. Caspi is also development lead and project director of Transportation Data Equity Initiative, which launched at the University of Washington in 2021 with an $11.45 million, multiyear award from the US Department of Transportation. The initiative is working to develop data standards for not only sidewalks but also transit centers and paratransit, including on-demand shuttles and community transportation on tribal reservations.[5]

A team at the federal Bureau of Transportation Statistics has started work to add a layer of data about pedestrian infrastructure to its National Transportation Atlas database. But this project will rely on local jurisdictions to provide that data, which is why the work of the Transportation Data Equity Initiative to develop a standard, and the work of OpenSidewalks and other efforts to create updated sidewalk datasets, is so critical.

We can also use data to better understand the street environment and the impact of infrastructure choices, traffic volumes, and speeds on people walking, rolling, or biking. In 2012, the Mineta Transportation Institute in California developed a Bicycle Level of Traffic Stress (BLTS) metric to understand both the stress bicyclists experience navigating a route and how far out of a direct route they would have to go to avoid higher-stress corridors. In 2021, with support from Alta Planning, Washington State Department of Transportation (WSDOT) expanded beyond the BLTS analysis to create a pedestrian level of stress analysis for the state's active transportation plan. WSDOT notes: "For population centers in Washington, LTS is measured on a four-point scale ranging from LTS 1, which provides the lowest stress and is often considered suitable for all ages and abilities, to LTS 4, the highest stress locations that most people walking or bicycling will avoid unless absolutely necessary."[6]

After computing a level of traffic stress (LTS) score for all state roadways and intersections, WSDOT designated the roads with the highest LTS scores as "gaps" in the bicycle and pedestrian network. It then scored those gaps based on safety, equity, and potential user demand metrics and created a rough estimate of what it would cost to arrive at LTS 1 or 2 on state routes in population centers throughout the state.

Level of stress analysis isn't just about the comfort of the person walking, rolling, or riding, it's also about safety. WSDOT explains: "Even though stress is subjective, it is associated with quantifiable roadway characteristics that can be reliably measured. The combination of roadway characteristics that make up LTS also describe exposure to the potential for a crash. Importantly, the kinds of

roadways that receive a higher LTS score based on their characteristics are also those that have more pedestrian and bicyclist serious
injuries and deaths."[7]

*Take Public Ownership of Sidewalk Repair
and Maintenance*

Mapping gaps in our pedestrian and bike networks, and then mar-
shaling the resources to fix those gaps, is the foundation for making it possible for nondrivers to get where they need to go. While
most sidewalks in the US are in the public right-of-way, in many
communities, repairing sidewalks is the legal responsibility of the
adjacent property owner. Because sidewalk repair can be prohibi-
tively expensive, and the city rarely takes action to force property
owners to make repairs, inaccessible and dangerous sidewalks can
go unrepaired for years. To address this, in 2019, the City of Oakland started requiring sidewalk maintenance at a property's point
of sale.[8] Denver, after attempting a rotating loan fund to make
sidewalk repair more affordable to property owners, decided to
move in the direction of the City of Boston and assume public
responsibility for sidewalk maintenance and missing sidewalk construction. Advocates with the Denver Streets Partnership began
organizing and managed to pass a sidewalks levy in 2022 that will
provide the funding for Denver to repair and complete missing
sections of its sidewalks network in ten years, instead of the previously projected four-hundred-year timeline.[9]

Keeping sidewalks clear from plants, ice, and snow is also legally
the responsibility of private property owners in most jurisdictions
in the United States. Advocates with the Independent Living Center in Chicago, Access Living, partnered with Better Streets Chicago to collaborate on a #PlowTheSidewalks campaign to push
Chicago to change that.

"When you see a city running multiple large plows on the streets and piling snow into the crosswalks and bus stops, there's no more clear illustration of whose mobility matters—and whose doesn't," said Laura Saltzman, the transportation lead for Access Living. "Without usable sidewalks, any idea of an accessible transportation system collapses: accessible stations and buses don't matter if you can't get to the train or the bus in the first place." In July 2023, the campaign was successful in getting an ordinance passed to develop a sidewalk-clearing pilot program.[10]

Build Pedestrian Connectivity

There are too many communities where sidewalks simply don't exist. Even in the city of Seattle, nearly a quarter of our streets lack sidewalks.[11] Building sidewalks after the fact is expensive and more difficult politically, so we need stronger regulations to ensure that sidewalks are required in new developments. It's unacceptable to be building new housing, offices, schools, or medical facilities that are unreachable for nondrivers.

In rural areas, we need to build bike and pedestrian infrastructure, such as multiuse trails that parallel highways or rural roads. On the Yakama Nation, the tribal lands of the Yakama people in Eastern Washington, many community members lack reliable access to a vehicle. It's not uncommon for people to walk twenty miles into town along US Route 97, a rural high-speed highway. As a result, this is one of the deadliest corridors for pedestrians in the state. The Yakama Nation is trying to raise funding for its Heritage Connectivity Trails project that can connect communities on the reservation, offering not only recreational opportunities for tribal members but also critical transportation connections.[12]

Another example of multiuse trails offering rural connectivity exists in Washington's Methow Valley, where the nonprofit

Methow Trails began organizing in 1977 to create what is now the largest cross-country ski trail system in the United States, with over 120 continuous miles of groomed ski trails. In the summer months, many of the trails are used for mountain biking, walking, or running. As a nondriver, it's one of the few rural communities where I feel like I can travel independently, as I can safely get myself to the nearest grocery store or into town without having to skirt along the shoulder of a treacherous rural highway.

Methow Trails is currently coordinating with private and public landowners to expand the trail network farther south so it connects to the region's public school and can provide safe, off-highway access for students and other community members.[13] Unfortunately, because of the popularity of the trail network and access to outdoor recreation, housing costs in the Methow Valley have exploded, making living, and even visiting, largely unaffordable. Like walkable urban communities, walkable rural communities are in high demand, a clear demonstration that we need to be building sidewalks and trails everywhere so that safe pedestrian access isn't a privilege only available to the rich.

Design Bike Infrastructure that Works for Everyone

Drivers know how to navigate a freeway on-ramp because designs are standard across the country. The same should be true of bike lanes, curb bulb-outs, floating bus stops, and multiuse trails, so that people riding, rolling, and walking know what to expect and how to safely navigate an intersection.

As new traffic calming and cycling infrastructure ideas are tested, it's critical to seek out the input of disabled people. As appealing as it may be to do a "quick build" installation, it's important for planners to address accessibility, even for what is perceived as a small segment of the population. It is also strategic to include input from users to minimize opposition to projects that will ultimately keep us all safer. A successful example of this collaboration is the outreach to, and discussions with, the disability community by San Francisco Municipal Transportation Agency (SFMTA) planners around the removal of car traffic from the main road in Golden Gate Park in San Francisco. SFMTA then developed a plan to ensure that disabled people wouldn't lose access to the park as the city planned to open the road to people moving outside of vehicles.[14] Some of the leading work on pedestrian accessibility and bike infrastructure also comes from the Bay Area, including the 2017 *Guidelines for Accessible Building Blocks for Bicycle Facilities*[15] and the 2019 *Getting to the Curb* report developed by the Senior and Disability Action work group of the San Francisco Vision Zero Coalition.[16]

Require Vehicles that Are Safer for Everyone

There are many changes that could be made to vehicles to make them safer for other street users, especially with heavier electric vehicles on the roads and the loss of sight lines on taller vehicles. Rating vehicles on the safety impacts on people outside of vehicles, like Europe does, would help, as would charging more for vehicle registrations based on vehicle mass.[17] The loophole that exempts many large SUVs from fuel economy standards should also be closed.[18]

Right now, speed limiter technology exists in most big rigs, but it is not required to be enabled.[19] While ultimately we need dynamic speed governors in every vehicle, until that is politically feasible, requiring speed limiters in commercial trucks, and in government-owned vehicles as some local governments are implementing, is a step in the right direction.[20] Author Jessie Singer points out that in 1979, in an effort to reduce fuel consumption, the National Highway Traffic Safety Administration enacted a regulation requiring car, truck, and motorcycle speedometers to display a maximum speed of 85 miles per hour. This rule was repealed by Congress in 1995, and its reinstatement could be another small step toward normalizing slower speeds. And finally, safety improvements like automatic braking and pedestrian detection must be required in new vehicles.[21]

Bigger picture, we need to take a more systematic approach to safety and ask how we can design a system where the possibility of serious and fatal crashes is reduced. Relying on enforcement doesn't address the underlying risks of having heavy, large vehicles traveling at high speeds through the places we need to walk and roll. A "safe systems" approach asks how we can remove that risk by lowering speeds and creating physically separated places for vehicles and people walking/rolling/biking. At the same time, it's critical that we reduce the speed and distances people need to drive by making better land use and housing policies that allow more of us to live in places where we can meet our daily needs without having to get in a vehicle.

Make Transit at Least as Reliable as Driving

For many years, transit riders who lack the resources or ability to drive were referred to as "captive" riders (now we use the slightly better, though still condescending, term "transit dependent.") As outlined in Nicholas Bloom's 2023 book, *The Great American Transit Disaster*,[22] decades of racialized underinvestment and neglect have resulted in a second-class system that is, in most American cities, viewed as a social service for those unfortunate enough to lack access to a car. The view that transit is for those who don't have other choices, and therefore those of us who ride transit will take whatever we can get, still lurks deep within many conversations around transit funding and service. It's time to call out the racist, ableist, and classist undertones of this assumption and invest in transit so that it becomes the reliable, comfortable choice to get us where we need to go.

Make Transit Accessible

We need to make investments that respect the dignity of transit riders. This means investing in bus stops and transit centers that are comfortable and accessible, with well-lit bus shelters and benches set back from high-speed roads.

It's completely unacceptable that so many legacy rail and subway systems, which in many ways offer the most reliable transit service in the United States, remain inaccessible for people who need elevators to access the stations. The Bipartisan Infrastructure Law included $1.75 billion over five years for station updates, which will make a significant dent in the nine hundred stations across the country that remain inaccessible.[23] But this is the bare minimum.

Compare the amenities provided to people in airports or the roadside service areas provided by state DOTs along major highways to the lack of amenities of any sort at most bus transfer stations or transit centers in the US. Bus riders also need bathroom facilities, water, charging outlets, and a place to get a cup of coffee or a candy bar. Many transit centers aren't staffed, which can make it more uncomfortable to wait or to get help if you're facing harassment or have a question about routes or where to wait for a bus. Yes, staffing takes resources, but when we compare the resources that go to staffing our airports or other public facilities, it's clear that it's a question of whose comfort and safety we are prioritizing.

Transit is also easier and less stressful to use when we have information about schedules and schedule changes that is reliable

Figure 3-1: Braille signage on a bus stop in Washington State's Skagit County.

Image Description: A bright green Braille and tactile sign with a bus stop number is affixed to a metal pole that sits in a grassy field with snowy mountains in the background.

and accessible in multiple formats (for people who have mobile wireless access and for those who do not). Braille signage on bus stops is important, especially if the bus stop lacks a shelter and there would be no other way for a rider to distinguish between the bus stop pole and a utility pole.

Better coordination between transit agencies and the transportation or public works departments who are responsible for sidewalk conditions is also critical. Dr. Beverly Scott served as the GM/CEO of four regional transit agencies: the Massachusetts Bay Transit Authority, the Metropolitan Atlanta Rapid Transit Authority, Sacramento Regional Transit, and the Rhode Island Public Transit Authority. When she started her career, she used to fight for all the funding she could get for transit specifically. But, she shared, "I started to get wiser. We have to look at the whole picture—the 'trip' and the purpose. In the first instance, most people are pedestrians. If we don't have the lighting, if we don't have the safety features, if we haven't arranged our overall public and private space to be accessible, then it really doesn't matter whether you got the shiniest bus or the newest train."

Increase the Reliability of Transit

As important as all of these amenities are, it is most important that transit runs frequently, reliably, and goes where we need it to go.

Carlos Aramayo is the president of Unite Here Local 26 in Boston, which represents hotel, food service, and casino workers. He is the fourth consecutive president of his union who has served on the board of the Massachusetts Department of Transportation (MDOT). "We are there because of our members' reliance on transit and the need for transit to get to work," Aramayo shared. He estimates that 80–90 percent of the union members commute via transit. "If you rely on transit to get to work, you can literally be forty-five minutes later than you think you're going to be," Aramayo said.

Dedicated bus-only lanes are a relatively low-cost solution to improving transit reliability and creating more service for riders without having to purchase more buses or pay for additional staff hours. A bus driver could complete a route and then repeat it in the same amount of time it would take a bus stuck in traffic to serve the route once. It's incredibly frustrating to be stuck in traffic on a crowded bus and look out the window at a sea of single-occupancy vehicles. Having experienced this frustration on many a Bx-12 Fordham Road "express" bus trip, nothing gave me more joy than seeing the Metropolitan Transportation Authority's GIF showing a bus lane–blocking car vaporizing to announce the new automatic ticketing system for vehicles blocking bus-only lanes.[24]

As a union that represents a transit-reliant workforce, Local 26 has successfully fought for more lenient time and employment policies because of challenges with transit reliability, which have increased as the Boston system has struggled with a backlog of deferred maintenance. Employers ultimately agreed to more flexible policies because they realized they would lose good employees by penalizing people who were late because of unforeseeable and unavoidable transit delays. Most employees aren't fortunate enough to have unions to negotiate policies like this, but it would benefit everyone if more employers formally recognized that employees who use our country's often unreliable bus or train system should not be penalized when they have less control over their arrival times.

Fund Transit

When asked what would improve their access, nondrivers in Washington State asked for more bus routes and more reliable

Figure 3-2: The Bx12 bus in New York, stuck in traffic.

Image Description: A view from the inside of a city bus through the bus window. Outside the window, cars are stopped in traffic.

schedules, weekend service, and lower fares.[25] The challenge of how to increase service levels while at the same time decreasing the financial barrier of using transit is frequently debated in transit advocacy spaces, and the "right" answer may be different based on how much, and what percentage of an agency's operating budget comes from farebox recovery.

First, there's no question that for some low-income community members, even a few dollars' fare can be a significant barrier. A pilot program in which King County Metro fully subsidized transit fare for very low-income individuals found that people with this ability to travel free of charge more than doubled their trips.[26] Tamara Jackson, policy analyst and legislative liaison for the Wisconsin Board for People with Developmental Disabilities, notes that "building public transit capacity and funding the operation of transit has been historically devalued, and there is a perception that users should foot the bill. For many low-income workers, increasing fares puts even public transit out of reach."

However, administering low-income fare-reduction programs takes resources. The documentation needed to qualify for these programs can also be a barrier to participation. This overhead, the inevitable exclusions, and the racialized impacts of fare-enforcement policies are good reasons to move away from relying on fare collection to fund transit systems.

It is also the large systems that rely most on fares to fund operations that are struggling the most in the post-pandemic era, including the transit systems in Boston, Los Angeles, San Francisco, Philadelphia, Washington, DC, Chicago, and New York City. In an April 2023 report, TransitCenter explains, "Transit agencies are facing a financial triple whammy—one-time payments from COVID-relief funding are drying up, fare collection has stabilized at well below pre-pandemic levels, and expenses are growing because of inflation, tight labor markets, and supply chain disruptions."[27]

To address this fiscal cliff, the Biden White House proposed temporarily allowing transit agencies to spend federal dollars for operations instead of the usual restriction to spend it only on capital projects. Most federal transportation funding flows through the states, and state transportation departments can and should allocate a larger percentage of their budgets to transit. The National Campaign for Transit Justice, managed by the Alliance for a Just Society and involving national organizations, including TransitCenter, Transportation for America, and the Natural Resources Defense Council, along with dozens of local transit advocacy groups across the country are advocating for new federal, state, and local funding sources for transit.

For local communities wanting to better fund transit, possible funding sources include raising parking rates, a tax on downtown employers, and road pricing. Transit levies are another option, but if anti-tax voters are a majority, relying on local support could leave some communities out, regardless of the fact that many people in that community can't drive or can't afford to drive.

In Seattle, where voters supported property tax increases to fund transit service in 2020, 68 percent of households live within a half mile of transit. But in Tacoma, Seattle's southern and historically more working-class neighboring city, anti-tax voters in more rural parts of the transit district rejected the most recent transit funding measure in 2012, resulting in only 4 percent of households having reliable access to transit.[28]

Increased state and federal funding for transit service, tied to requirements for service levels, could help reduce disparities between wealthier and more liberal communities where levies to fund transit are typically successful and those where transit levies had failed or never been brought to the voters. In Washington State, Front and Centered, Disability Rights Washington, and our allies secured funding from the state legislature for a frequent transit standard study in 2022. This study, completed in 2023, compared transit service levels across the state and outlined scenarios and funding levels that would bring frequent transit service to communities whose current transit service levels leave many nondrivers stranded.[29]

As "choice" riders abandoned transit at the start of the pandemic, commuter routes saw their ridership vanish, while routes serving working-class, Black, and Brown neighborhoods retained riders who didn't have the option to work from home or drive themselves. This pattern repeated itself all over the country. The Urban Institute reported that in Denver, routes that served lower-income neighborhoods actually saw an increase of riders between 2020 and 2021.[30] These pandemic shifts in ridership made visible how many people can't easily, affordably, or reliably get where they need to go by driving themselves, and how "essential" it is for us to prioritize transit service that exists outside of rush-hour, weekday trips.

In response to the pandemic and post-pandemic changes in transit ridership, many agencies are moving away from clustering service around rush-hour trips, routes, or schedules that too often ignored the needs of people with nontraditional work schedules or people making other trips outside of work commutes. But a shortage of transit workers, such as bus drivers and mechanics, is limiting the ability of many systems to rebuild service levels post-pandemic, much less expand service where it's needed. According to a 2022 TransitCenter report, almost three-quarters of transit agencies across the US cut or delayed service because of worker shortfalls. The main reason cited for these shortages was

that transit operator jobs are no longer attractive, primarily because of the skyrocketing cost of housing and other cost of living
expenses. The report noted that "operator assaults have increased,
rigid scheduling requirements make it difficult for junior operators
and workers with child or eldercare responsibilities, and a lack of
access to adequate facilities—both restrooms on route and break
rooms at depots—exacts a health toll on operators." TransitCenter
recommends transit agencies offer better compensation and paths
for advancement, as well as ensuring workers have more control
over schedules and working conditions (see the section in chapter 4, "Hire Nondrivers and Support Nondrivers in Leadership
Roles").[31]

Invest in Intercity Routes

We can't forget about intercity routes. As part of the 2021 Bipartisan Infrastructure Law, the USDOT is looking into the feasibility
of increasing long-distance Amtrak routes, including the restoration of the North Coast Hiawatha service that ran from Chicago
to Seattle through southern Montana and was discontinued in the
late 1970s.[32] Increased intercity bus service and new and restored
long-distance passenger rail lines will also help people in more
rural parts of the country access services in larger cities.

We often hear that it's infeasible and impractical to provide transit service in rural areas, but school buses already serve very rural
routes. In rural areas of the Pacific Northwest, it's not uncommon
to see small huts at the end of driveways for children to wait for
the school bus in comfort. It is time to recognize that adult rural
nondrivers need to have a transit option too. The private school
bus industry is protected from competition from public transit by
the "Tripper Rule," which prevents public transit agencies from
offering routes that specifically serve public schools.[33] With driver

Figure 3-3: A hut for students to wait for the school bus on a rural road in Washington.

Image Description: A cedar shingle hut with a bench and small window at the end of a driveway on a rural, forested road.

shortages impacting both school transportation and public transportation agencies, maybe it's time to rethink these restrictions and create more routes that serve the needs of all nondrivers.

Understand When On-Demand Rides Make Sense

The limitations that are placed on paratransit riders should be reconsidered, such as the required twenty-four-hour prescheduling or the inability to make changes to pickups. Paratransit riders often deal with the frustration of delayed rides. There's no reason that with the technology that exists for scheduling and routing our paratransit systems can't be improved. Many agencies are making these investments, though securing sufficient funding for the updates, and for enough drivers and vehicles to serve riders in a timely way, is always a struggle. Some agencies have experimented with outsourcing some paratransit rides (those that don't require a wheelchair-accessible vehicle or "hand-to-hand" assistance getting to a destination) to ride-hail companies, which can provide the service less expensively. But we need to ask how much of this is because of the gig-economy model, which doesn't sufficiently compensate the ride-hail drivers for the real costs of operating or subsidizes those costs with venture capital funds.[34]

People who rely on nonprofit transportation providers for prescheduled rides would benefit from updated scheduling and routing programs to make it easier to schedule trips. Staci Sahoo and her team at Hopelink in Washington State have been building an online system that allows people to see which transportation providers serve their area and the requirements or limitations to their service and then allows them to book a trip. Sahoo believes that outreach from trusted community members, especially in languages other than English, is key to making seniors and other nondrivers in those communities aware of transportation options.

Her hope is that this new scheduling tool and more inclusive communication strategies should help nondrivers who can't be serviced by paratransit or transit gain new mobility.

In rural and lower-density areas, on-demand transit that replaces some fixed-route service might make sense. But if the idea is to design a system that is convenient and affordable, which will draw more users, it's important for planners to think about how it will scale, both in cost and in the ability to deliver reliable service. Metro Micro, a publicly funded, on-demand shuttle pilot in Los Angeles, costs four times as much as fixed-route transit to operate.[35] Metro Micro users are more likely to be younger, and more likely to be female, than bus riders, with some riders expressing that they feel safer scheduling a pickup than using the bus. In Wilson, North Carolina, where the city replaced its entire bus fleet with publicly funded microtransit, riders who felt that riding the bus was too stigmatizing were more willing to give public transit a try.[36]

Some on-demand ride companies have made accessibility for disabled community members a priority. However, barriers still exist for riders who may be accustomed to using fixed-route buses to switch to these systems, including language and technology access barriers, as well as other unanticipated access needs. In 2019 when the on-demand "microtransit" provider Via came to my Seattle neighborhood, I couldn't use the service with my two-year old because there was no way I could carry a thirty-pound car seat once I got out of the Via minivan and onto light-rail. After many rounds of communication with King County, who contracted with Via for its services, I was told that neither the county nor Via would be able to provide car seats because they couldn't find a car seat that would meet their insurance requirements. I was also told that since Via operated under taxi laws, I technically was allowed to ride with my child without a car seat, but every time I tried to do so, drivers would try to refuse us. Riding in a vehicle without a car seat also didn't feel particularly safe.

Eventually, from other parents in the blind community, I learned about a harness designed as a more portable securement system for small children. I bought one and started using it whenever I knew we would need to get ride hail or Via. But it made me question why the car seat industry only seems to be interested in manufacturing car seats built for private use in personal vehicles. Why are there not more easily portable options or options designed to meet insurance requirement for use in shared vehicles? And why haven't car manufacturers designed built-in options? Especially as we are seeing more purpose-built robotaxi prototypes, it's important to remember that young children, and caregivers with young children, need to go places too.

I was also fortunate that Via wasn't my only transit option, and I could either take a local bus to transfer to the light-rail or walk the mile to the nearest station. What if I was a parent or caregiver of a young child who lived in a city like Wilson, North Carolina, that replaced its whole fixed-route transit system with Via vans? Every day, riding the local bus through my neighborhood, I see other parents and grandparents with young kids. If microtransit and ride hail exclude young children, how can these systems actually work as a mobility "solution" for communities?

Caregivers with young children aren't the only people excluded from on-demand rides. Lack of wheelchair accessibility, and/or the cost of these services, excludes many nondrivers. It's important to think about the larger transportation context in which these public-private partnerships, or private (often venture capital–funded) transportation companies operate. What if the company decides it isn't profitable to operate in a region or a neighborhood? Is the provider cherry-picking the most cost-effective clients to serve, leaving fewer options for people who need wheelchair-accessible vehicles or who are traveling with children? What if the company uses up its venture runway, can't turn a profit, and disappears (as we've seen with countless ride-hail, scooter, and bike-share startups)? And what are the broader societal impacts on vehicle miles driven, on congestion, and on driver wages and working conditions?[37]

Paris Marx, author of *Road to Nowhere: What Silicon Valley Gets Wrong about the Future of Transportation*,[38] believes that venture capitalists aren't thinking about how to make our communities more accessible but instead are "just responding to grievances they have with the system." As a result, the mobility solutions proposed by tech companies don't address the needs of low-income or disabled people. But having different people in the room designing more inclusive tech solutions isn't enough. "Ultimately, I don't think we're going to really solve any of these problems, if the government is not stepping in and making serious investments to improve transportation. And it doesn't matter how many new technologies we deploy, that reality is not going to change," Marx concludes.

All of the barriers, exclusions, and negative externalities of ride hail will likely be repeated if and when robotaxis are ever widely deployed. Additionally, the same biases we see in AI systems trained on datasets that underrepresent non-White and disabled people apply to the intelligence of these automated vehicles, exposing those of us already more likely to be walking, rolling, or biking along our public right-of-ways to greater risks.[39] Bigger picture, if driving becomes easier, how will this impact our land use and travel patterns? Will we see even more spread-out communities, longer distances between destinations making it all but impossible to get where we need to go without paying for a ride? Already, we have built the places we need to go too far away from the places we can live or afford to live. We shouldn't pretend that reliance on ride hail (autonomous or other) is getting us closer to communities without car dependency.

Provide More Equipment Types, Storage, and Charging for Everyone Who Wants to Bike, Scoot, and Roll

Our infrastructure investments must go beyond places to ride; we must also plan and invest in secure places for people to store and charge mobility devices. New apartment complexes, schools, and commercial spaces should be required to provide secure bike parking. When in-building parking isn't feasible because of stairs or space constraints, building owners should be required to provide secure outdoor parking options, like bike cages or bike storage. Bike parking must be designed to work for a wider range of bike types, not just two-wheel bikes that can be easily lifted into vertical storage options.

Nondrivers need more roll-on, flexible space options on transit that would fit a broader range of cargo bikes, recumbents, and scooters. Caltrain's bike cars in the Bay Area, Southeastern Pennsylvania Transportation Authority's bike cars in Philadelphia, and roll-on bike storage on the Swift bus rapid transit lines in Snohomish County, Washington, are examples. While bringing bikes on transit isn't always feasible, secure and affordable storage lockers or bike cages that fit larger devices are an absolutely essential public investment. There are new types of secure bike-parking containers available, such as Ooneepod, and some transit agencies are investing in secure bike lockers that can store larger bikes.

Public permitting for micromobility should mandate inclusive scooter and bike share to accommodate parents, caregivers, and

Figure 3-4: Roll-on bus bike parking, Snohomish County, Washington.

Image Description: The interior of a city bus with two bikes racked at a 45-degree angle by a system of rollers and hooks.

disabled people. It is encouraging that shared e-bikes and scooters with sit-down options are increasingly available for everyone to use in these systems. As of spring 2023, communities that mandate or incentivize seated scooter options include Bloomington, Seattle, Berkeley, Pensacola, and Milwaukee.[40] New York City, Oakland, and Berkeley require that shared-scooter operators provide for rent an adaptive wheelchair vehicle or an e-power attachment that can be affixed on a manual wheelchair to give the user more range or the ability to go up hills more easily.[41]

Over the summer my five-year-old was discovering the freedom of riding his own bike, I rented an electric "sit-down" Veo scooter for my dad, who is pushing 80. He had not been on a bike in years and wouldn't try a stand-up scooter, but he loved chasing his grandkid along the lakefront in Seattle on the Veo. At a dollar a minute, I ended up chasing my dad down the park trying to get him to cut off the ride before I racked up an unaffordable charge. Even when the shared devices are accessible, it's unlikely that many lower-income disabled people could take advantage of these shared scooter options given the rates have risen as the venture capital–funded companies try to make a profit. In response, communities like Buffalo, Oakland, and Burlington are experimenting with e-cargo bike–lending libraries, specifically for low-income community members.[42]

Providing more affordable trikes, recumbents, e-bikes, and cargo bikes for purchase will also mean more people can get where they need to go. Rad Power Bikes' investment in an affordable e-trike could be a game changer for people wanting the extra balance support. Colorado offers income-based e-bike rebates, with larger credits available for e-cargo bikes and adaptive e-bikes. California, Connecticut, Hawaii, Massachusetts, Rhode Island, Washington, and Vermont also offer statewide e-bike incentives.[43]

Too often, the default is to use sidewalk space for bike and scooter parking, creating conflict when bikes (especially wider bikes) block sidewalks, or when undocked scooters and shared bikes are left scattered over the sidewalk, blocking access and creating tripping hazards. Bike and scooter parking can be created in the right-of-way, perhaps used to daylight intersections and make it safer for crossing. Milwaukee, San Diego, Washington, DC, and Seattle have all experimented with the installation of bike- and scooter-share corrals to keep bikes and scooters from clogging sidewalks. When possible, bike- and scooter-share companies should have docked parking so that shared devices can't be left by users or knocked over in ways that block accessibility and create tripping hazards. Where undocked systems exist, shared-micromobility companies must do a better job about ensuring that users don't leave devices blocking pedestrian access. Until this issue can be resolved, cities should not continue to permit dockless shared-bike and scooter companies.

In addition to e-bikes, we need to legalize bigger-than-bike but smaller-than-car options, think golf cart–speed devices with cargo- and passenger-carrying capacity and perhaps some protection from the elements. Transportation journalist David Zipper has written about how the Atlanta suburb of Peachtree has embraced the golf cart, and it could be exciting to see how other communities adapt to an increase in seniors who are aging out of driving but want to maintain their mobility.[44] Currently golf carts are illegal to operate on most streets in the US, but with a reduction in speeds of all vehicles, it could be safe and possible for vehicles of this size to operate on our roadways. Especially if licensing requirements don't exclude youth and disabled people, golf cart–sized, speed-limited vehicles could expand mobility options in communities where the distances between destinations are too far to walk or roll without

Figure 3-5: Scooter- and bike-parking corral in Seattle with sit-down Veo scooters.

Image Description: A series of bike racks in a parking spot between the road and a bike path. Parked in the "corral" is a traditional stand-up scooter, Veo brand scooters that look more like mopeds with built-in seats, and a large e-cargo bike.

e-assist, which unfortunately is the case in all but the densest parts of our oldest cities in the United States.

Embrace Remote Access and Delivery

While remote access to participate in work, school, conferences, and social activities may have peaked during the pandemic, it should continue to be an option. Having the option to telework, get telehealth, and participate in community activities remotely allows people to be involved when travel is a burden, too risky, too time consuming, or too expensive and also helps reduce carbon emissions.

As employers began to rehire after the initial pandemic layoffs, in many cases making telework an option for the first time, disabled workers had new job opportunities. In research published in late 2022, Ari Ne'eman, a doctoral student in public health at Harvard, found that from the last quarter of 2021 through the second half of 2022, employment gains by disabled people outpaced employment gains for nondisabled people by 14 percent. Ne'eman explains: "Closer examination of the occupations where disabled employment growth has exceeded that of non-disabled suggests that these trends are not solely attributable to tight labor markets but may also be shaped by the structural shifts in the workforce brought about by COVID-19, in particular the shift towards telework."[45] This is backed up by the Bureau of Labor Statistics, which found that in 2022, a greater percentage of disabled people were employed than in any previous count.[46]

Jenelle Landgraf is a low-vision mom who lives in Leavenworth, a small mountain town a three-hour drive from Seattle. Before the pandemic, to get to her job as a clinical social worker she had to commute to Wenatchee, a larger town in the region. If she could drive, it would have been a manageable thirty-minute commute, but on rural transit the trip took an hour and a half on the bus each way, and she had to rely on her husband to drive her from their home to the nearest bus stop because her rural road doesn't have sidewalks.

When I first interviewed Landgraf, she told me, "The long bus commute is one of the reasons I probably will choose not to keep working in Wenatchee. But there are a lot more job opportunities for me in Wenatchee than in Leavenworth. There's only one clinic here in town for me to work at if I want to keep working in mental health." But as telehealth became widespread, she was able to start seeing patients remotely and avoid the long commute. It was a huge relief for her to be able to work without spending hours and hours every day trying to get to an office.

Because medical appointments are one of the more difficult destinations for nondrivers, telehealth can be a gamechanger, not just for medical professionals but also for people seeking care. The Department of Veterans Affairs is one of the leaders in broadening medical access, offering home-based primary care, telehealth, and community-based outpatient clinics.[47]

Private providers are also expanding remote health care and home-based care options. When I was struggling to get to urgent care within an hour of where I live in Seattle, a friend told me about a program called DispatchHealth that launched in 2013 and offers at-home dialysis and urgent care services.[48] I haven't tried using its services yet, but next time I have a kid that's too sick to spend an hour on the bus, rather than calling 911, I'm grateful to have another option.

Ensuring every household has remote access will require us to continue to invest in municipal broadband and to continue to insist that software and hardware companies develop accessible products that can work for people with the full range of sensory, physical, and cognitive disabilities.

Online shopping for durable goods as well as groceries and meals should be available to people who need it, not just those with high incomes. This may require subsidies or publicly supported services because low delivery costs shouldn't come at the price of underpaid delivery and overworked warehouse workers. Workplace health and safety regulations must be enforced at Amazon and other online retailers, and worker organizing respected. It's important these rights and protections are also extended to subcontracted delivery van drivers, who are also under intense pressure to speed up deliveries, at the risk of their safety and the safety of others.[49]

For gig delivery workers, the safety risks are significant, and workers across the country are organizing for better working conditions and better pay. In New York City, Los Deliveristas Unidos organized the city's sixty-five thousand food delivery workers and have won regulations that will raise their hourly rate to $23.82 by 2025.[50] In 2022, organizers with Working Washington successfully fought for legislation that requires contract workers to earn the city's $17.27 minimum wage and be reimbursed for mileage at the federal rate.[51] And in March 2023, Seattle was the first major city to make COVID-era protections for gig delivery workers permanent, requiring companies like DoorDash, Instacart, and Uber Eats to provide paid sick time.

Approach Housing, Transit, and Services as an Ecosystem

For our towns and cities to work for nondrivers, we must reduce the distances people need to travel to go to the places they need and want to go. This means building housing with greater densities and making sure the zoning laws and parking requirements incentivize, rather than discourage, the location of retail, groceries, offices, health care and childcare facilities interspersed with housing rather than in separate areas that can be reached only by driving.

The concept of the fifteen-minute city has been circulated in planning conversations since the 2010s and began to be adopted as a policy objective by city governments across the world as pandemic restrictions reduced travel. At a fundamental level, fifteen-minute cities are a reminder that it is possible and beneficial to build cities so that car travel isn't necessary to meet our daily needs. And while I don't love the name—fifteen-minute cities implies that there is a homogeneity around how long it takes people to walk or roll a set distance, which simply isn't true—the underlying concept is key to making communities work better without driving.

In his role as the policy director for Seattle City Councilmember Tammy Morales, low-vision nondriver Devin Silvernail worked on an update to Seattle's Comprehensive Plan so the city would allow commercial or nonprofit groceries, fresh healthy food merchants, childcare, health services, home goods, and cultural anchors in residential neighborhoods, if existing services were more than a quarter of a mile away.[52] Neighborhood retail is much more common in older neighborhoods, and corner stores continue to offer vital services in many communities throughout the US, but too often retail, childcare, and other essential services are zoned out of newer housing developments. These Seattle Comprehensive Plan revisions could begin to rebuild what we lost when we restricted anything but housing in residential neighborhoods.

Reform Parking

We also must remember that prioritizing car parking and car access to locations not only makes driving the easier choice but also makes arriving somewhere by walking, rolling, or riding more difficult. Drive-through and drive-through-only businesses are an obvious target for reform. In 2018, Portland, Oregon, passed legislation requiring that drive-through-only services allow people to access the drive-through window as pedestrians or cyclists.[53]

Other communities, including Minneapolis and Long Beach, have banned new drive-throughs because of their impacts not only on pedestrian safety but also on car traffic congestion and air pollution.[54] This is an important shift from what we encountered during the pandemic, when many businesses, as well as COVID testing and vaccine clinics, were accessible only as drive-throughs, a public health mistake when the reality is that nondrivers also need to access care and many did not have someone in their household who could drive them.[55]

Car parking also creates barriers for nondrivers, not only when we have to cross large hostile parking lots to access businesses in suburban, strip mall–type developments, but also when planners choose to allocate limited public right-of-way space to car parking instead of wider sidewalks, bus priority lanes, or protected biking infrastructure.

"Often, people try to pit parking reforms against people who need disabled parking spots," explains Cassie Wilson, a wheelchair user and climate and mobility justice advocate from Oregon. "We can have both parking reform and access for people who need disabled parking spots by converting regular parking spaces to disabled ones and making sure they have the recommended space for people using wheelchairs to exit the vehicle safely."

With less parking, more drivers will be encouraged to take transit, walk, or roll and to seek out closer businesses that don't require them to drive and park. This is the kind of market shift we need, but it will be almost impossible to achieve when driving yourself in a private vehicle remains by far the most convenient choice.

Build Abundant Housing

"Growth management" laws that seek to limit sprawl can help to ensure we are building higher-density housing instead of building low-density housing on the cheapest land that is far away from existing services, disconnected from transit routes, but without changes to allow and incentivize more density, the lack of new housing construction has made too many of our communities un-affordable to all but the wealthiest.

Additionally, growth management legislation has too often come with transportation "concurrency" ordinances that require local jurisdictions to maintain vehicle level of service—measured in sec-onds of delay or inconvenience to drivers, even during peak travel periods—even as new housing or development is permitted.

Chris Comeau is a senior transportation planner with the Transpo Group and has worked with local jurisdictions in Wash-ington State for more than two decades on land use and trans-portation planning. He explains how concurrency has resulted in local governments widening roads and intersections to ensure that vehicular levels of service, even at the busiest time of day, remain at a static level.

Comeau worked as a transportation planner for the City of Bell-ingham during the housing boom in the mid-2000s, when, be-cause of a concurrency threshold violation, the City of Bellingham put a moratorium on new development on a major commuter cor-ridor since evening rush hour traffic congestion was getting worse as the city grew.

In 2008, Bellingham realized that, instead of just measuring vehicle level of service, it would stay in compliance with the con-currency rule if it came up with a new methodology that measured the movement of people—including people riding bikes, walking, and riding transit—not just the movement of cars. With this new multimodal level of service methodology, the city was able to build higher density infill housing and grow in compact mixed-use ur-ban centers connected by transit.

"It injected a huge amount of capacity into the citywide trans-portation system because it went from auto only to multimodal,"

Comeau shared. It also meant that the city could stop widening roads and intersections in response to traffic congestion, which, Comeau notes, "was completely counter to the goals that we have for pedestrian safety because as the intersection got wider, the crossing got longer."

In the 2023 legislative session, Washington adopted the multi-modal level of service into an update to the state's growth management act, requiring cities and counties to ensure that the needs of transit riders and people walking, rolling, and biking are weighed along with the needs of drivers.[56] It is still to be seen how this will be adopted, as planners have yet to reach consensus on reliable methods for measuring the movement of people outside of vehicles.

There is also the inherent tension between "level of service" measurements that look at how fast and how many people move, and the reality that congestion might actually keep us safer by reducing speeds and help us prioritize which trips are important.

From his experience in Bellingham, Comeau believes much of the most difficult work is in convincing the public that reducing congestion shouldn't be the overarching priority of local government. He insists we need leaders who are willing to be straightforward with how our communities must change:

> We're gonna densify. There's going to be more people living here in the future, and we need you all to get ready. That includes more traffic in certain places, and you're going to have to get used to it. We're not going to widen our streets just because it's not as easy to drive anymore. We want it to be easy to walk. We want it to be easy to bike or get on a bus or cross the street to a bus stop. Nobody enjoys traffic congestion, myself included. But that's literally the trade-off for focusing on density and people-oriented infrastructure. You cannot continue to make it easy to drive or park a car if you're trying to plan for people.

In addition to redefining expectations around traffic volumes and speeds to counteract arguments against growth and density, we also need to continue to change our zoning laws to allow more homes. Many local jurisdictions are working to add "missing middle" housing by passing laws that make it easier to build more units per lot or even to legally split lots to allow additional housing construction and ownership. Oregon passed a law in 2019 that allows duplexes on single family–zoned lots across the state, and Vermont, California, and New Hampshire have statewide accessory dwelling unit laws allowing owners to build another residential structure on their property. While missing middle housing is an important infill strategy, our cities also need additional investment in higher-density housing to ensure that we are building at scale and can ensure housing affordability in places where market rents far exceed the incomes of many community members. Transit-oriented development (TOD) policies that allow greater densities and taller buildings near high-frequency transit, especially TOD developments that are publicly funded or on publicly owned land, can provide some of this scale and affordability. And we need to fund and legalize structures so that low-income and middle-class people can afford stable housing, whether that be through social housing initiatives, affordable unit requirements, rent-control and tenant-protection laws, land trusts, or housing co-ops.

At the end of the day, best practices evolve, and we experiment with new policy ideas. While the concepts highlighted in this chapter will hopefully be useful for some time in the future, the key to creating communities that work better for nondrivers is to listen to nondrivers. Nondrivers must be incorporated into the decision-making and daily operations of the structures that govern our land use and transportation systems. The next chapter includes a range of suggestions on how to do so.

Valuing the Expertise of Nondrivers

IN THE FALL OF 2021, I was invited by Roger Millar, the head of the Washington State Department of Transportation, to speak to the board of the American Association of State Highway and Transportation Officials (AASHTO) at its annual meeting in San Diego in 2021. Before the meeting, Secretary Millar briefed me, explaining that I'd be presenting to the heads of each state department of transportation, and I started to get really nervous. I am not a civil engineer. I don't have a degree in urban planning, and I have never worked for a transit agency or department of transportation. What I had was my lifetime of experience as a disabled nondriver and stories from the hundreds of other nondrivers from every corner of Washington State. I believed that because of that experience, I had knowledge and experience that people who have driven their whole adult lives do not.

But everything that I had experienced about our transportation system up to the time of this presentation made me doubt that I would be taken seriously. I felt it every time I tried to make my way across an eight-lane arterial, skirted bushes and mud puddles inching my way down a road without sidewalks, or sat stuck on a bus with other frustrated travelers in a traffic jam of mostly single-occupancy vehicles.

As I stepped into the cavernous conference room in the San Diego Convention Center, I anticipated an icy reception. Four long tables had been arranged in a square, around which sat the board members. Behind them, along the edges of the room, staff listened and took notes. I took a seat behind Secretary Millar and figured that perhaps I'd get some polite applause at the end of my presentation and then a quick pivot to the next agenda item.

I started my presentation with a video featuring many of the people who appear in this book, showing how they get around, talking about the barriers and gaps they encounter, and their dreams for communities where their needs are considered. As the video concluded and I started my presentation, I could tell the room was engaged. Perhaps for the first time, agency leaders from across the country were being asked to consider how the transportation systems they build and maintain impact the mobility of nondrivers. They were reminded that nondrivers exist, that there are a lot of us, and that the experiences I was sharing from Washington State mirror those of people in every community in every state represented in that room.

"When you were able to come in with the stories, and with the startling conclusion that 25 percent of Washingtonians don't drive, that really resonated," Secretary Millar told me afterward. He said colleagues were texting him while I was talking, reporting that they'd asked their staff to look into how many nondrivers exist in their states.

Highlighting that nondrivers constitute such a large percentage of our population, and that our communities built around driving are not meeting their needs, was further reason for leaders like Millar (who served as the president of AASHTO in 2022–23) to push for a new and different vision for transportation.

For climate advocates who want to ensure we are investing in the kinds of policies that will reduce emissions, a focus on the mobility needs of nondrivers can also be a useful frame. "Reducing climate emissions at the scale and speed we require means we have to change how we design our communities and get around. Electrification won't be enough," insists Mike McGinn, director of the national pedestrian advocacy group America Walks and former mayor of Seattle.

Before he was elected mayor, McGinn was chair of the Washington State Chapter of the Sierra Club. This experience informed McGinn's deep commitment to decarbonizing transportation. Because of our abundant supply of hydropower in the Northwest, our largest carbon emitter is, and has been for many decades, the transportation system.[1] McGinn points out that as the rest of our country moves away from coal-powered plants, the percentage of emissions from transportation will increase, and decarbonizing transportation will become more central to our national climate commitments.

When I first met McGinn, I had just moved to Seattle and started representing Disability Rights Washington at a coalition meeting of groups working on transportation issues. At first, I was really annoyed at this guy who always arrived on a bike and squeezed his large frame, along with his helmet and bike panniers, into the corner of the crowded conference room. He kept saying he wasn't there as part of any group. Why was he invited? And why was everyone else letting him take up so much space, both in the physical room and in the discussions?

After a couple of meetings, I started to notice that I found myself agreeing with him more often than not. In a room of people who always wanted to make sure we had the right data or the right policy statement, he seemed to understand that what we really needed was to mobilize a broader base. I asked him to coffee to strategize. It was shortly before this meeting that I realized that Mike was actually Mike McGinn, Seattle's former mayor, who served from 2009 to 2013.

"Politics runs on power, and those defending and benefiting from the status quo have power," explains McGinn. "Whether those directly benefiting from the billions spent on road expansion or those who have their transportation choices and convenience deeply subsidized, not just by dollars, but by the lost lives, lost health, and lost opportunity of those most damaged by overbuilt roads and pollution. To beat that kind of entrenched privilege and power takes more than white papers, it takes organizing."

And we need to mobilize a political base, because unfortunately, those in power are advocating for electrification alone as the way to decarbonize the transportation system. Rather than putting resources toward figuring out how we can lower emissions by reducing the distances and frequency we need to travel, or the size and weight of vehicles we travel in, or investing in mass transit, the electrification of our private automobile fleet offers a way for much of the status quo to be preserved. It's also a win-win for automakers, who benefit from generous electric vehicle subsidies that will drive more demand for new vehicles.

Paulo Nunes-Ueno was also skeptical of a transportation decarbonization strategy focused solely on electrification. He was the transportation lead for Front and Centered, a Washington State coalition of environmental justice organizations with Black, Indigenous, and People of Color (BIPOC) leadership. In the summer of 2020, Front and Centered conducted listening sessions with member organizations about transportation justice, and one thing that came across loud and clear was that the low-income and BIPOC groups, who continue to face disproportionate harms from automobility, were seeing little benefit from the electric vehicle subsidies that only wealthy people could afford to use.[2]

"Black and Brown communities face more air pollution and less connectivity because they were bisected by highways," Nunes-Ueno explained. "We are asking the same people to bear the price of these racist policies again and again." By funding the construction and widening of highway infrastructure through primarily low-income Black and Brown communities, Front and Centered argued that our transportation investments were continuing to harm communities that have disproportionately borne the high environmental and public health costs of automobility.

Working together, Front and Centered and Disability Rights Washington began to insist that our transportation investments reflect the needs of our communities and that we stop widening highways and expanding road capacity. Decarbonization should benefit everyone. We needed our state to invest in more reliable transit service and in the sidewalks and safe places to walk and roll so that people can get where they need to go, even if they cannot drive.

After two years of advocacy, in 2022, the Washington State legislature passed a $17 billion transportation package that included $5.2 billion for transit and bike and pedestrian projects. For the first time, these "multimodal" investments were larger than the amount the package allocated for highway capacity expansion. It also included a complete streets mandate, directing WSDOT to include bike and pedestrian facility construction in state highway projects with budgets greater than $500,000 that are in areas identified in the state active transportation plan or local plans as deficient for people walking, rolling, or riding. (Because of this mandate, in 2022 WSDOT estimated that nearly half of all road-way projects scheduled to start between 2022 and 2028 require the construction of bicycle and pedestrian facilities as part of the project to address gaps in accessibility.)

"Having your voices, the voices of nondrivers, at the transportation committee hearings transformed the conversation around transportation funding priorities," shared state senator Rebecca Saldaña, who served as the vice-chair of the senate transportation committee. "We were used to hearing from lobbyists and people in the industry. And for the first time, we were hearing from people who were being impacted by the inequities in our transportation system. That had a profound impact on the investments we were able to make for walking, rolling, and transit."

The 2022 Move Ahead Washington transportation package wasn't everything. It still included far too much funding for highway capacity expansion projects, projects that will lock us in to a future of auto dependency. But it showed that by building coalitions led by people excluded from and harmed by our decisions to prioritize car mobility above all else, those priorities can be shifted.

Help Transportation Professionals to See beyond the Car

"Most engineers are drivers, that's what they've grown up in, driving around town. You have to start changing that perspective," explains Kristina Swallow, director of Tucson's Planning and Development Services Department and former director of the Nevada Department of Transportation.

Swallow made a point of walking, biking, and riding the bus to work. In what she called her "director's challenge," she asked each member of her executive team to walk, bike, or use transit once a week, for a nonrecreational purpose, and report back on what they experienced making that trip. At their weekly meetings, she asked the team to spend twenty minutes discussing these experiences: why they thought a piece of infrastructure was designed a certain way, and what they could potentially do to make it more comfortable for users outside of vehicles.

These conversations influenced planning decisions: Swallow recalls working on the design of a state road through a rural community where the plan was for fourteen-foot lanes and a 25 mile per hour speed limit. She knew that no one would drive 25 miles per hour when the lanes were that wide, so she successfully pushed to narrow the lane width to slow speeds and use the extra space to create a large shoulder for safer pedestrian and bicycle access.

"We're dealing with people who have a car, generally. And that is the same across the country—it is the same class of people who are ending up being able to serve in these positions," explains Tamara Jackson, co-chair of Wisconsin's Non-Driver Advisory Committee. (As a reminder, the committee includes representatives from disability, senior, and bike advocacy organizations, regional planners, local government organizations, rural and urban transit systems, and state agencies who serve people more likely to be nondrivers. Denise Jess is co-chair with Jackson.) "Our end goal is that they're thinking about nondrivers, and we are helping them apply that knowledge to their work."

For each of the twice-yearly meetings, Jess and Jackson develop scenarios for small group activities. After the first session, Jackson remembers, there was a "sea change" in the attitude of members as they started to understand the complexity of the challenges nondrivers face and the things that nondrivers need. "There were definitely members of the committee who, at the beginning, were like, 'Why can't we just solve this with an app on our phone?' Or, 'Can't they get a ride from a friend?'" Jackson recalled. "But after we did the scenario, we didn't hear those questions anymore."

In one scenario, the group looked at a decision to move a hospital in Milwaukee from downtown to a location closer to the interstate, which improved access for drivers. The committee members discussed how this move made access much more difficult for those patients and hospital service workers taking transit.

"We're creating a culture of folks thinking about nondrivers," Jackson explained. "When somebody who's spent their whole life in transportation realizes that they've built something that many people cannot use, we see the department [of transportation] really shifting how they see transportation to be much more comprehensive. They think they've been solving transportation problems through roads, and when they realize that there are lots of people who can't use those roads, they really want to design a system that does what they think it does."

Include Disability Perspectives in Education and Training

We also need urban planning and engineering schools to teach students about accessibility and the needs of nondrivers. Maddy Ruvolo, who in 2020 earned a master's degree in urban planning, shared, "My planning school curriculum contained nothing about disability. I think we were supposed to do a day on paratransit in one of my classes, and then we fell behind schedule and didn't cover it, or anything else related to accessibility."

A report by the National Center for Mobility Management published in 2022 backs up Ruvolo's experience. "Several of the faculty explained that the national licensure and credentialing bodies, such as Engineer in Training (EIT) certification program driven by the Accreditation Body of Engineering (ABET), are very specific regarding the course content that can be offered. Therefore, it is difficult to find time to adapt the curriculum to fit in content regarding disability and mobility management."[3]

In this report, Judy Shanley, PhD, who co-chairs the Transportation Research Board Committee on Accessible Transportation and Mobility, makes a series of recommendations for schools: inviting guest speakers who are experts in disability; providing practical assignments for students to work with agencies that provide mobility services for nondrivers; and requiring students to explore the various plans that states are required to complete that address public transit, sidewalks, and human services transportation. She also recommends that schools do a better job of recruiting and supporting disabled students interested in careers in transportation.

Because disability access receives such little attention in transportation planning and engineering schools, other organizations have stepped up to fill this gap with continuing education programs. Technical assistance centers like the National Aging and Disability Transportation Center and others who work under cooperative agreement with Federal Transit Administration offer trainings and resources for people in the transportation sector to learn everything from how to support youth transitioning into adulthood plan for mobility options to best practices for working as a paratransit or mobility program manager.[4]

Conduct a Walking/Rolling Audit

A walking/rolling audit of existing infrastructure or the proposed project area can also serve as an important tool for planners, engineers, and elected leaders to understand the gaps in access and what changes are needed to make a street work better for people outside of vehicles. This is especially true of the walk/roll audit conducted in partnership with community members with disabilities who can point out how the infrastructure is, or isn't, meeting their needs. As a starting place, the AARP has developed a walk audit toolkit,[5] and the National Association of Chronic Disease

Figure 4.1: A group of transportation engineers and planners on a walk/roll audit, led by Abby Griffith.

Image Description: A Black woman with a white cane leads a group of adults along a sidewalk.

Directors offers a multiday Walkability Action Institute for local planners and engineers.[6] Jonathon Stalls also offers thoughtful tips for organizing walking group activities in *Walk: Slow Down, Wake Up, and Connect at 1–3 Miles per Hour.*[7]

"Inside lingo from planners or engineers isn't nearly as effective in making the case as someone's personal experience just trying to get somewhere," Barb Chamberlain, director of Active Transportation for Washington State Department of Transportation, explained. "When we talk about something as basic as whether a person can cross the road to reach the other side and whether the traffic feels too fast and scary to try, everyone can relate to that. And then we can talk about what this means as a barrier to simply living everyday life if you're someone who can't drive, who needs those crossings to be there every single time."

In the summer of 2023, I partnered with WSDOT to coordinate the participation of disabled community members in a series of walk/roll/bike tours across different regions in our state. At the first of the tours, which took place in a rural, agricultural community, I joined a group of engineers and planners as we saw both the good—a trail connection that safely connected users over an overpass and across an off-ramp—to the questionable—a hairy slip lane we had to navigate to get to the transit center. It was encouraging to hear the transportation professionals listen to the problems highlighted by the community members and wrestle with how they were going to make the community and their projects work better for people walking, rolling, and riding. It was work they were excited to do, and while there are still decades of work to get us to a place where nondrivers can safely and comfortably navigate this community we toured, I know the work is starting.

Help Elected Officials to See beyond the Car

Many of the same tools will work for elected officials (such as the walk/bike/roll audit mentioned above). But having elected officials hear directly from constituents and experience what nondrivers experience can be especially powerful.

In 2014, I was hired by the hotel workers union in Washington, DC, to film mayoral candidate Muriel Bowser as she spent a morning shadowing one of its members who worked as a housekeeper at a downtown hotel. We met the housekeeper at her home, caught a local bus, and then transferred to the Metro. As we paid the transfer fee to board the Metro, I remember Bowser having a conversation with the housekeeper about the financial burden of this fee, which penalized low-wage workers who couldn't afford to live near the Metro and needed to transfer from the bus system (in 2021, the Washington Metropolitan Area Transit Authority finally got rid of the transfer penalty).[8]

In the summer of 2021, when I started to think about how Disability Rights Washington could help elected leaders better understand the barriers nondrivers experience, that conversation was the genesis behind the Week Without Driving Challenge.

The challenge is simple: participants have to try to get around for a week without driving. They can take transit, walk, roll, bike, or ask or pay for rides as they try to keep their regular schedules— attending to their work responsibilities, campaign obligations, grocery runs, kid transport, and social activities.

In 2022, we had more than four hundred participants from across the state, including WSDOT secretary Roger Millar. We even received an official proclamation from Governor Jay Inslee that underlined the connections between our work to improve the accessibility for nondrivers with climate and environmental justice goals.[9] The following year, we partnered with America Walks to bring the challenge to communities across the United States, with participation from more than 142 host organizations from forty-one states.

We encourage participants to learn more about the barriers disabled nondrivers experience by speaking with disability organizations or disabled individuals in their communities. In Washington State, we have facilitated conversations between elected leaders and disabled constituents from their city or district about what it is like to get around without being able to drive themselves, where the nondriver constituents offer tips for the elected officials on route planning and trip preparation.

That additional time needed for route planning and preparation surprised many participants. Pierce County Councilmember Jani Hitchen reflected, "It changed my whole life. I had to think about how do I pick up dog food for my very large dog that eats a lot. How do I get to work every day and make sure that I can move around safely? I had to think about when I can leave, how I get there, what I'm going to wear."[10] State legislator Emily Wicks found herself slipping off her heels and walking barefoot to be able to walk down a steep and slippery section of sidewalk.

Others were caught off guard when bus routes stopped running, and they found themselves having to ask for favors to get rides. Everett City Councilmember Liz Vogeli found out the hard way that the bus route she'd relied on didn't run past 8:00 p.m. on Sundays. She had to go back to the community event where she had been and ask for a ride.

I understand it is much easier for participants who have the privilege to live in an area well served by transit, with connected sidewalks or bike infrastructure. Or if they can work remotely and outsource their driving and other transport and delivery needs to

Figure 4-2: During a Week Without Driving event with elected officials, Krystal Monteros points out a missing sidewalk connecting the bus stop to her apartment complex.

Image Description: A Latina woman in a wheelchair wearing a Disability Mobility Initiative T-shirt speaks to a group of people wearing blazers who are standing on a narrow sidewalk next to a wide road.

other people. In asking participants to reflect on the challenge, we ask them to consider how race, age, wealth, immigration status, and caregiving responsibilities shape the experience.

Even for participants who might already bike, walk, or take transit for some of their weekly trips, we've heard that the experience has helped them comprehend the difference between taking the easy trips and taking *all* trips without driving. King County Council Chair Claudia Balducci said, "I'm a person who chooses to travel mostly by using my bicycle and transit. And I thought when I was invited to participate in this event last year, that it would be pretty easy. But I learned right away that it's a lot different to choose to not drive versus to not be able to drive. And in fact, going through a week as if I was unable to ever drive myself or my family, and had to rely entirely on other means of transportation, taught me a lot about how our system works and doesn't work."[11]

Also of note, some of the most poignant reflections came from participants who "failed" at the challenge and ended up grabbing their keys and driving. Pierce County Councilmember Marty Campbell faced a medical emergency in his family and ended up driving every day of the challenge in 2022 to get to medical appointments. As he was sitting in his vehicle, Campbell told me, he had a lot of time for reflection: "If I didn't have access to a vehicle, how would I have gotten here? How long would it have taken? Or could I even reach the destination?" He now is very interested in ensuring there are transit stops near all medical facilities, not just the major hospitals.

Elected leaders who participated also came to see the ways nondrivers might become isolated or miss out on community connections when mobility becomes a significant burden. Many elected officials expressed how uncomfortable they felt asking friends or colleagues for rides, especially for trips that felt discretionary, such as for social gatherings. Larry Goldman, councilmember from Lake Forest Park, shared, "I feel awkward asking someone, can you give me a ride to go out to eat at this restaurant with some friends?" Paula Rhyne, a councilmember from Everett, described feeling "a little bit blue" by the end of the week because she'd forgone so many social activities.[12]

After participating in our Week Without Driving challenge for two consecutive years, Councilmember Neal Black from Kirkland, Washington, reflected, "It's kind of hard to imagine how someone who didn't have access to a car could do the job of a city council member. Our expectations are to be in a lot of different places, and a lot of different times. In a suburban city like ours, it's a challenge to do that without driving, and that means there's a large segment of our population excluded from serving in this role."[13] Black's reflection really gets to the heart of the problem: our expectations around the roles of elected leaders, combined with communities based on automobility, make fulfilling those expectations as a non-driver nearly impossible—unless you can afford a personal driver.

"This week was a reminder that mobility is a human right. And it's also a reminder that so many people in our region are excluded from this right, simply because driving for them is not an option," shared King County Councilmember Girmay Zahilay.[14] Zahilay is a champion for transit and for safer crosswalks, fighting for funding to build missing sidewalks and to reduce speeding cars and improve pedestrian safety in the unincorporated community of Skyway, where heavy freight traffic and decades of underinvestment have resulted in little pedestrian infrastructure.[15]

As the Week Without Driving expands to more communities throughout the United States, Zahilay offers a promising example of how to use the experience to highlight the inequities in transportation and accessibility. I can't wait for more elected leaders to have a chance to experience how difficult it is to get where they need to go safely and comfortably as a nondriver, and to see how this experience will impact their commitment to fighting for the transportation funding and land use policies we need.

Agencies Need to Learn How to Share Power

"Nobody knows their neighborhoods, their communities, and their needs better than the individuals who are experienced in it," insists Dr. Beverly Scott. "You must plan with, not for, people and not for communities. There is absolutely no substitute."

Changing who has the opportunity to be in these rooms—in charge of transportation departments, running public transit agencies, setting transportation research agendas—won't happen overnight, but there are steps everyone currently in these spaces can take to ensure they are listening to, and prioritizing, the needs of people who don't have that privilege.

After a decades-long career in the transportation industry and her leadership of half a dozen transit agencies, Dr. Scott has now largely turned her focus to public service and a nonprofit she founded, Introducing Youth to American Infrastructure (Iyai+). Dr. Scott explains that the Iyai+ mission is to "inspire historically underrepresented youth to pursue careers in critical infrastructure sectors, including transportation, and pushes the importance of meaningful youth voices in problem identification, problem-solving, and decision-making within their communities."[16]

"It's shameful that we've got all these people with gray hair sitting at decision-making tables when we are talking about 2050 planning horizons," Dr. Scott insists. "The people that are making decisions for the most part will be dead by the time that any of it comes to fruition. And so, it is not a matter of altruism. It is not a matter of oh, I'll make two tables here, and you get to be at the little table, and we're gonna be at the big table. This is a matter of responsibility on the part of those who are being good leaders and stewards."

Despite all the rhetoric about equity and inclusion and listening to the next generation, when it comes down to changing who gets to provide input and how that input is valued, too often the people in decision-making roles still fundamentally believe they know what's best and are unwilling to value community input.

"When you're in a position, are you humble enough to know when the time is to use your positional power to make space for other people?" asks De'Sean Quinn, assistant general manager of partnerships and strategy at King County Metro.

Quinn was tasked by Metro to help convene a mobility equity cabinet, which I was invited to be part of in 2019. Our task was to help shape a mobility framework that would guide the long-range planning process and service guidelines for the agency.[17]

"When we talk about sharing power, that's what it actually looks like," Quinn reflected on what ultimately made the Metro Equity Cabinet different from other experiences of community input that left people feeling tokenized. "The people who are furthest away from the decisions also have a role to play in helping us surface solutions."

With guidance from the Greenlining Institute, King County Metro worked to support community participation, providing stipends for our time, free childcare, and meals during meetings. Most importantly, it felt like our input was guiding the priorities of the agency, especially as we were able to highlight the needs of the diverse communities we represented and make sure those needs, and those communities, were being considered in both the research informing the plan and the priorities of the agency going forward.

Most controversially, the cabinet recommended shifting resources from high-frequency, high-ridership routes that primarily served tech worker commuters to service that would serve lower-density, lower-income areas of the county where more low-income, non-White, and transit-dependent people live.

"A real reflection of how important our work was: all the things that we recommended, the travel trends that we looked at, came true during COVID," Quinn reflected. The high-frequency commuter routes were more or less abandoned, while ridership on the routes servicing lower-income areas of the county, the areas we had asked Metro to prioritize, were still full of riders who needed to get to work, to the grocery store, to doctor's appointments.

Dr. Rosalie Ray, assistant professor at Texas State University, studied the creation of the King County Metro Equity Cabinet as a leading model for power sharing in transportation decision-making. Aside from the concrete task of developing the mobility framework, Dr. Ray noted that the equity workgroup clearly served as capacity building for the participants: "You all learned how to better advocate, how the government processes worked, and how to advocate for the changes or resources your communities needed, and many of you went out and shared that within your networks."

And while I was excited to see our framework shape the future of the transit agency, it was this capacity building that had the most impact for me. Being in that room, being compensated to be there, and provided with childcare and meals and the large-print handouts I needed to see the content in the PowerPoints, made me feel for the first time that I actually had valuable knowledge about our transportation system. As a low-vision person, a parent, and someone who relies on the bus system, there were things I knew about how to make it work better, knowledge that no one else in that agency had, despite their degrees or credentials. While my decision to organize and support nondrivers to become transportation leaders has many origins, the King County Metro Equity Cabinet was an important influence.

Hire Nondrivers and Support Nondrivers in Leadership Roles

Imagine a highway department staffed entirely of people who do not drive. Maybe they ride as passengers in cars sometimes, or drive when out of town on vacation, in other countries where more people drive, where driving is easier, more comfortable, and more convenient. Our perspective of what a transportation system should look like would be heavily influenced by what people walking, rolling, and taking transit need. Would we be able to know what would work best for drivers at a highway interchange? Probably not, and yet the inverse of this is the reality for most of the people in charge of our transportation system, to the point where it's still revolutionary to suggest that engineers or planners get out of their cars and try walking or biking a road project to experience how it works for people outside of cars.

We are all limited by our own experiences of the world, and no matter how many planning degrees or expensive consultants are involved in a project, it's users of the system, especially users who don't have other options, who will be able to give the most important input about what works and what is needed. So, while all the solutions presented in the previous chapter are important, what is most fundamental, and in the end presents the greatest opportunity for true transformation, is ensuring that nondrivers, and in particular nondrivers from communities historically excluded from power, get to be the ones deciding the future of mobility.

"'Who decides' and 'who rides' are often very different, in three important ways: geography, gender, and race," according to a 2022 TransitCenter report.[18] The report found that transit boards and agency leadership do not reflect the demographics of transit ridership. The report also notes that frontline transit workers are excluded from decision-making leadership roles and voting power on transit boards. "Instead," TransitCenter notes, "service planning decisions are typically made by management and transit planners, roles in which White and college-educated people tend to be overrepresented."

"Because many on these boards tend to be car drivers, they really haven't internalized what it means to be a transit rider," Judy Jones explained. Jones is blind and has relied on transit her whole life. She says that the transit board "may make wise decisions regarding budgets but they really don't feel it in the gut as a transit rider. Those decisions determine whether you, as a transit rider, are going to be able to keep a job, continue to be a caregiver, continue to go to school."

Jones serves as the chair of the Skagit Transit Community Advisory Committee and has been a transit advocate for many years in both Florida and Washington. Although she has found contact with individual board members to be positive, she is excluded from the board work sessions, which means when it comes to discussing budgets, even as the chair of the Community Advisory Committee, she's out of the room. Some transit agencies are structured differently to ensure that transit riders have a voice in decisions. In Washington, Intercity Transit, which serves the state's capital city and surrounding region, has a nine-person board that includes local elected representatives, a labor representative, and three "citizen" representatives who are also full voting members.[19] Justin Belk, one of the citizen representatives and the vice-chair of the board, shares, "I feel incredibly lucky that Intercity Transit has citizen representation with a voting seat at the table. While the elected officials are there for a reason, we offer a different perspective."[20]

For some nondrivers, having reliable transit or paratransit is the difference between being able to live in community and being forced to move into an institution like a nursing home. For others, it means being able to get to places without having to call in favors, to have each wish to go somewhere judged and evaluated by someone else. This means that nondrivers tend to care deeply, passionately, about having transit work for us, to a degree that people who have more mobility options may never feel. And because transit, walking, and rolling usually take more time than driving, we have spent countless hours considering our transportation, land use, and housing decisions and what changes, big or small, we wish could be made to have it work better.

Both this passion and these countless hours of contemplation are legitimate reasons transit agencies and the transportation sector more broadly should hire and work with nondrivers. There are potentially a lot of disabled nondrivers who are unemployed or underemployed and would be eager to have the opportunity to share this hard-earned knowledge. According to the Bureau of Transportation Statistics, only a fifth of working-age adults who are disabled work full- or part-time. Over three-quarters of non-disabled adults are employed.[21]

"As the transit industry faces workforce challenges, the timing seems right to consider untapped hiring pools that include potential applicants with disabilities," stated the 2022 report on disability and higher education for transportation professions by the National Center for Mobility Management. "Our nation's transportation planning preparation departments have an important role in shaping the future of the transportation workforce. This workforce should and must include individuals with disabilities."[22]

"I think we desperately need more disabled folks in urban planning and transportation planning," shared Maddy Ruvolo, who works as a planner for the San Francisco Municipal Transportation Agency. While Ruvolo emphasized how important it was to have external advocates asking for (and demanding) a more accessible environment, she said that she also found it incredibly valuable to have city staff with their own experiences of disability on the project teams and in the rooms where changes were being debated.

An easy step for employers is to stop requiring driver's licenses for jobs where driving isn't an essential function. This one seems pretty simple, but I find driver's license requirements all the time on new transportation planning, admin, and engineering postings. Someone explained once that a driver's license requirement was a default setting on their internal HR system for job posts, and so until those HR settings are turned off, it will be the default on every new posting.

Having a driver's license isn't the only unnecessary exclusionary requirement. I have had a transportation department insist that yes, it was important that a transportation planner be able to carry forty pounds because they might need to attend a community outreach event and transport a box of outreach materials. Yes, if you're disabled you can apply for the job and, once you have it, approach your new boss and ask for an accommodation, but knowing how to negotiate that (or even being granted a useful accommodation) isn't guaranteed.

It's time for employers, and in particular employers in the transportation sector who would like to learn more from the expertise of nondrivers, to comb through the standard HR language on job postings and think about how much of it is necessary and where it is only excluding or discouraging candidates unnecessarily. Agencies must also consider what kind of knowledge and expertise they are leaving on the table when they prioritize planning degrees over lived experience from people who rely on transit and depend on walking and rolling to get where they need to go. Change will take more than hiring a disabled or BIPOC person with an urban planning or engineering degree—it means figuring out how to bring people into decision-making roles, into employment or compensated community participation, people who haven't had the chance to go to college, to pursue unpaid internships, to speak the language of transportation planners.

"There are people who are going around with a checklist of the ADA requirements, but you don't have people with different disabilities in the room when you're designing these things," disability advocate Erica Jones explains. "Part of that problem is the economic system we have requires full-time availability from people to have a job at all. And so, you find that if you can't work forty hours or you can't work thirty hours, you might as well be able to work zero hours. And so, a lot of the disabled people who should be in the room when you're designing these things are people who only have the energy for ten or fifteen hours a week of work, and so those people have zero chance of getting into the room."

In addition to people who can't sustainably work a full-time schedule, there are other disabled people who, in order to qualify for Medicare coverage from the state for their complex medical needs, can't be paid for more than ten or so hours of work a week. Even if offered a job with full health benefits, those benefits rarely cover the actual care they need, and so to stay alive, some disabled people must choose to limit paid work.

If we're going to make transportation systems, and our communities more broadly, work for everyone, we need to rethink the underlying fallacy that you are only as valuable as the hours you can work, and look toward the work of disability justice activists who are challenging employers to rethink how we structure work requirements and workplaces to allow more people to contribute their expertise.[23]

Conclusion

As TRANSFORMATIVE AS CAR DEPENDENCY HAS BEEN, we have to remember that it wasn't always this way.

After my son was diagnosed with the same neurological vision condition I have, I kept getting questions about whether anyone else in my family had nystagmus. And I couldn't fully answer, because so many of my family members in my great-grandparents' generation, including my namesake great-grandmother Anna, had died in their teens or early twenties in the influenza pandemic, before they ever would have had the opportunity to own or drive a car. (Family lore is that another one of my great-grandmothers was so terrified of automobiles, she got a tattoo of a rose on her hand so if she was killed in a crash they would be able to identify her body.)

Someone in this generation could easily have had nystagmus, or another condition that prevented them from driving, and it wouldn't have been as life defining as the inability to drive is now, when car ownership and a driver's license have become both a symbol and a requirement of productive adulthood.

"The proliferation of driving and the glib equation of mobility with mobility by car actually excluded an enormous fraction of the population," explains University of Virginia historian Peter Norton, author of *Fighting Traffic: The Dawn of the Motor Age in the American City* and *Autonorama: The Illusory Promise of High-Tech Driving.*[1]

Initially, automobility was embraced mostly by wealthy, White men, who were the primary beneficiaries as suburbia, highways, and car dependency became signifiers of progress. We don't give as much consideration to who was left out. Not just people who couldn't physically drive, but people who couldn't easily afford cars, and for whom vehicle ownership was, and continues to be, a financial stressor, Norton reminded me.

"A lot of people who had been well served by walkability, by buses, by streetcars, by commuter rail lines, passenger rail—found themselves worse off," Norton elaborated. "Some of that population could switch to a car, sometimes with a lot of financial hardship because it's a lot more expensive. But for a lot of that population, switching to a car was not a practical option."

Before the rise of automobility, cities in the United States had the density to support public transit. As Nicholas Bloom points out in *The Great American Transit Disaster*, new zoning policies, often driven by the desire to prevent poor and Black people from moving into suburban communities, lowered housing densities to the point that transit could no longer function without heavy subsidies.[2] Bloom also points out that as public transit became integrated in the United States, car-dependent suburban communities and large investments in car infrastructure were funded so that White people could remain segregated. Automobility was driven by, and continues to enable, a refusal to share public space.

This context is important to remember when we question and

start to push back against car dependency. We must recognize that we are calling into question a system that, at least in the short term, serves the interests of the people with the most power and wealth in our society. Untangling ourselves from a dependence on mobility based on driving is not going to be easy. It's going to take organizing the biggest, most powerful coalition of people for whom automobility doesn't work. And that coalition should be centered on the needs of, and led by, nondrivers, who are the most deeply vested in rethinking a system that doesn't work for us.

"There's no argument that is going to suddenly persuade people to do the difficult, morally correct thing," explains author Jessie Singer. She reflects on how the auto industry knew that steering columns were impaling and killing people in crashes, and even though they held the patent on collapsible steering columns, it took another ten years until Ralph Nader and the consumer protection movement he led forced automakers to change. "The way you move the levers of power is by pressuring risk-averse politicians. Those politicians are never going to do anything that is uncomfortable for them unless you make it uncomfortable for them to not act. And rallying people power to push those public figures is the only way anything ever gets done."

This organizing starts with being visible. Washington State Department of Transportation secretary Roger Millar kicked off the 2023 Lifesavers Conference on Roadway Safety by reminding attendees that 25 percent of the population can't drive or can't afford to drive and that it is the role of transportation departments and others in the industry to see nondrivers as constituents too, whose needs and safety are just as valuable as those of people traveling in cars.

We start with this visibility, and we organize for more power.

Former Seattle mayor Mike McGinn reflects: "It took us decades to make us car dependent, and too many people think we now have no other choice. But this system was not brought down from the mountaintop by Moses. We built it, we can change it, and the best time to start is now."

Will it be possible to undo the harms of automobility, both the physical infrastructure and the cultural norms that have become our status quo over the last century? Being a parent of a child who will also not be able to drive, I have to believe it is possible. I also believe it is necessary.

As the sky turns orange, the storms get stronger, and the waves higher, we are reminded of the immediacy of the threat and the moral prerogative to disrupt failed mobility and land use systems that are locking us into decades of carbon emissions. We also need to be reminded of the immediate daily and cumulative public health and environmental harms from tire dust, noise pollution, and traffic violence/enforcement, harms that wealthier, Whiter, nondisabled people are largely able to avoid. But those of us who can't drive, because of disability, age, or income, see every day how automobility is failing us. And we also believe that it must be changed. With our guidance, and a recognition of this leadership, we can and will create a different future.

What You Can Do Right Now

Many of the recommendations in this book are actionable by people who work in the transportation sector or serve as elected leaders. But even if you feel powerless to influence decisions about land use, housing, and transportation, there are steps that you can take to move us toward a world that works better for nondrivers.

Shift Modes

- Reduce the number of trips you take by sharing trips, combining trips, and planning in advance.
- Switch some trips you would normally take by car to a different mode. Can you walk or roll instead of driving? Can you take the bus? Even though it will take longer, you can enjoy the time and read your kid a book!
- Remember the school drop-off paradox. When you choose to drive, you make it more dangerous and less comfortable for other kids to access school or activities without a car. Consider how parents and caregivers who can't drive get to the activities

you take your child to. Is there a nearby transit stop? Is there a well-lit sidewalk? Is there bike parking?

- Mode shift may also mean changing the places you go. Instead of going to the park or the grocery store on the other side of town, what would it mean to stick to more local options?
- Get to know your immediate neighbors and find activities that you may be able to participate in locally.
- Take the Week Without Driving challenge and encourage your friends, colleagues, and elected officials to do so as well.

Treat the Sidewalk Like a Highway

- Keep the sidewalk in front of your house, apartment building, or business clear of snow and leaves and other clutter like signs, garbage cans, or shared bikes or scooters.
- If you use bikes or scooters and you need to park on the sidewalk, make sure not to block curb ramps and that your parking job is not making the sidewalk too narrow for someone in a large powerchair to get through. Some blind people who use white canes will use the edge of the sidewalk and the adjacent building wall as guidance, so it's much better to park in the parking strip between the street and the sidewalk than along a building wall.
- If you're a property owner in a city where it's your responsibility to repair the sidewalk adjacent to your property, make necessary repairs. If it is not financially or logistically possible to make repairs, coordinate with your city and your neighbors for help.
- Many people who are blind rely on hearing to navigate urban spaces. Quieter vehicles, including bikes and scooters, can be much harder to detect. This puts an extra onus on bike and scooter users to always yield to pedestrians. You may not know if someone sees or hears you coming. Just as you as a scooter or

bike rider may feel vulnerable to large cars or SUVs, consider how the speed or closeness at which you encounter other users can feel threatening, even if you feel totally in control.

Plan for the Future

- If you're a parent or caregiver, use transit! Maybe you live somewhere where you can incorporate public transit trips into your daily or weekly schedule, or maybe it's only feasible on special trips to bigger cities. Either way, it's important to teach kids to use transit and to navigate places walking or rolling.
- If you're planning to move, when looking for a home, take into consideration how accessible a potential new apartment or house is to transit or if it is possible to walk, bike, or roll to the places you might need to go. Consider prioritizing freedom from car dependence over other factors, for yourself and for other people in your household.
- Plan for aging out of driving safely, and if you have parents or other elders in your life, help them plan. Consider how basic needs will be met without driving. It may involve a family support network, learning how to ride the bus, getting an e-trike or e-bike, and/or getting connected with social services that provide rides. If it is an option, consider moving to an area with more essentials within walking, rolling, or transit distance.
- Vote for levies or other tax measures to increase funding for sidewalks and transit. Vote for elected leaders who will support these investments.

Step Back to Make Space for Other Voices

- Ask yourself how you can step back and create space for people who don't usually get the chance to be in the room or to be heard. Examine what perspectives and what access to resources you bring to the table. Question who is not in the room or who isn't being taken seriously in a decision-making process. Even when you may feel relatively powerless as a junior staffer or as a volunteer advocate, it's important to examine who will be impacted by the work you're doing and if the people most impacted by these decisions are having meaningful input. Noticing who isn't in the room is the first step. Next you can ask, What would it take to change this?

Notes

Foreword

1. Mike Maciag, "Riding Transit Takes Almost Twice as Long as Driving," *Governing*, January 26, 2017.

Preface

1. Disability Mobility Initiative, Disability Rights Washington, "Transportation Access for Everyone Storymap," accessed March 1, 2023, https://www.disabilityrightswa.org/story map/.

Introduction. Despite What You Think, Not Everyone Drives

1. US Department of Transportation, Policy and Governmental Affairs, Office of Highway Policy Information (OHPI), "Highway Statistics 2020," modified September 24, 2022, https://www.fhwa.dot.gov/policyinformation/statistics/2020/.

2. OHPI, "Highway Statistics 2020."

3. Evelyn Blumenberg, Anne Brown, and Andrew Schouten, "Auto-Deficit Households: Determinants, Travel Behavior, and the Gender Division of Household Car Use," February 28, 2018, https://rosap.ntl.bts.gov/view/dot/63059.

4. US Census Bureau, "Vehicles Available," https://www.census.gov/acs/www/about/why-we-ask-each-question/vehicles/.

5. Washington State Legislature Joint Transportation Committee (WSLJTC), *Nondrivers: Population, Demographics, and Analysis* (N.p.: Toole Design, Cascadia Consulting Group, and Strategic Research Associates, 2023), https://leg.wa.gov/JTC/Documents/Studies/Nondrivers%202022/NondriversStudyFinalReportSummaryReport.pdf.

6. WSLJTC, *Nondrivers.*

7. Todd Littman, "Evaluating Active and Micro Mode Emission Reduction Potentials," Transportation Research Board 2023 Annual Meeting: TRBAM-23-03449, December 12, 2022, https://www.vtpi.org/amerp.pdf.

8. Seattle Department of Transportation, *2019 Surveillance Impact Report: Acyclica* (Seattle: City of Seattle, 2019), https://www.seattle.gov/documents/Departments/Tech/Privacy/SDOT%20Acyclica%20Final%20SIR.pdf.

9. Washington State Department of Transportation, "Active Transportation Plan," https://wsdot.wa.gov/construction-planning/statewide-plans/active-transportation-plan.

10. Alexandra Murphy, Alix Gould-Werth, and Jamie T. Griffin, "Validating the Sixteen-Item Transportation Security Index in a Nationally Representative Sample: A Confirmatory Factor Analysis," *Survey Practice* 14, no. 1 (October 2021), https://doi.org/10.29115/sp-2021-0011.

11. Alexandra K. Murphy, Karina McDonald-Lopez, Natasha Pilkauskas, and Alix Gould-Werth, "Transportation Insecurity in the United States: A Descriptive Portrait," *Socius* 8 (January 2022), https://doi.org/10.1177/23780231221121060.

Chapter 1. Nondrivers Are Everywhere

1. Washington State Legislature Joint Transportation Committee (WSLJTC), *Nondrivers: Population, Demographics, and Analysis* (N.p.: Toole Design, Cascadia Consulting Group, and Strategic Research Associates, 2023), https://leg.wa.gov/JTC/Documents/Studies/Nondrivers%202022/Nondrivers StudyFinalReportSummaryReport.pdf.

2. WSLJTC, *Nondrivers*.

3. Bureau of Transportation Statistics, "Travel Patterns of American Adults with Disabilities," September 2018, https://www.bts.gov/travel-patterns-with-disabilities.

4. Center for American Progress, "Advancing Economic Security for People with Disabilities," July 26, 2019, https://www.amer icanprogress.org/article/advancing-economic-security-people -disabilities/.

5. Pamela Loprest and Elaine Maag, *Barriers to and Supports for Work among Adults with Disabilities* (Washington, DC: Urban Institute, 2001), https://www.urban.org/sites/default /files/publication/61576/410107-Barriers-to-and-Supports -for-Work-among-Adults-with-Disabilities.PDF.

6. Office of Disability Employment Policy, *Disability and the Digital Divide: Internet Subscriptions, Internet Use and Employment Outcomes* (Washington, DC: United States Department of Labor, 2022), https://www.dol.gov/sites/dolgov/files/OD EP/pdf/disability-digital-divide-brief.pdf.

7. Meghan Miller, "Removing Obstacles for Disabled Workers Would Strengthen the U.S. Labor Market," Center for American Progress, May 24, 2022, https://www.americanprogress.org/article/removing-obstacles-for-disabled-workers-would-strengthen-the-u-s-labor-market/.

8. Bureau of Transportation Statistics, "Travel Patterns of American Adults with Disabilities."

9. EyeWiki, "Driving Restrictions per State," January 5, 2023, https://eyewiki.aao.org/Driving_Restrictions_per_State.

10. Centers for Disease Control and Prevention, "Diabetes and Vision Loss," last reviewed December 19, 2022, https://www.cdc.gov/diabetes/managing/diabetes-vision-loss.html.

11. Centers for Disease Control and Prevention, "Prevalence Estimates—Vision Loss and Blindness," May 2021, https://www.cdc.gov/visionhealth/vehss/estimates/vision-loss-prevalence.html.

12. Rebecca Vallas, Kimberly Knackstedt, Hayley Brown, Julie Cai, Shawn Fremstad, and Andrew Stettner, "Economic Justice Is Disability Justice," Century Foundation, April 22, 2022, https://tcf.org/content/report/economic-justice-disability-justice/.

13. National Council on Disability, *2020 Progress Report on National Disability Policy: Increasing Disability Employment* (Washington, DC: National Council on Disability, 2020), https://ncd.gov/sites/default/files/NCD_Progress_Report _508_0.pdf.

14. Bureau of Transportation Statistics, "Household, Individual, and Vehicle Characteristics," United States Department of Transportation, December 21, 2011, https://www.bts.gov/archive/publications/highlights_of_the_2001_national_household travel survey/section_01.

15. National Equity Atlas, "Car Access," 2020, https://nationale quityatlas.org/indicators/Car_access#/.

16. WSLJTC, *Nondrivers*.

17. Food and Nutrition Service, "Study of the Food Distribution Program on Indian Reservations," US Department of Agriculture, June 2016, https://www.fns.usda.gov/fdpir/study-fd pir-8.

18. Alexander Butler, Erik Mayer, and James Weston, "Racial Disparities in the Auto Loan Market," US Consumer Financial Protection Bureau, March 31, 2021, https://files.consumer finance.gov/f/documents/cfpb_mayer_racial-discrimination -in-the-auto-loan-market.pdf.

19. Fines and Fees Justice Center, "Free to Drive," accessed August 10, 2023. https://finesandfeesjusticecenter.org/cam paigns/national-drivers-license-suspension-campaign-free-to -drive/.

20. Nina R. Joyce, Melissa R. Pfeiffer, Andrew R. Zullo, Jasjit Ahluwalia, and Allison E. Curry, "Individual and Geographic Variation in Driver's License Suspensions: Evidence of Disparities by Race, Ethnicity and Income," *Journal of Transport and Health* 19 (2020), https://doi.org/10.1016/j.jth.2020.10 0933.

21. Washington State Department of Licensing, "Statistics at a Glance," Calendar Year 2022, https://www.dol.wa.gov/sites /default/files/2023-06/2022-CY-stats-at-a-glance.pdf.

22. Insurify, "Hang Up the Keys: Cities with the Most Suspended Driver's Licenses," July 30, 2021, https://insurify.com/insigh ts/cities-with-the-most-suspended-drivers-licenses/.

23. Charles T. Brown, "Arrested Mobility," https://arrestedmobility .com/.

24. Sarah A. Seo, *Policing the Open Road: How Cars Transformed*

American Freedom (Cambridge, MA: Harvard University Press, 2019).

25. Kimberly Cataudella and Alexia Fernández Campbell, "Undocumented Immigrants Can Get Licenses—ICE Can Get Their Data," Center for Public Integrity, January 28, 2022, https://publicintegrity.org/inequality-poverty-opportunity/immigration/undocumented-immigrants-licenses-ice-data/.

26. Wendy Fry, "More than a Million Undocumented Immigrants Gained Driver's Licenses in California," *CalMatters*, January 27, 2023, https://calmatters.org/california-divide/2023/01/drivers-licenses-undocumented-immigrants/.

27. National Immigration Law Center, "How California Driver's License Records Are Shared with the Department of Homeland Security," December 2018, https://www.nilc.org/issues/immigration-enforcement/how-calif-dl-records-shared-with-dhs/.

28. National Equity Atlas, "Car Access."

29. Disability Mobility Initiative, Disability Rights Washington, "Transportation Access for Everyone Storymap," https://www.disabilityrightswa.org/storymap/.

30. King County Metro, *Mobility Framework Report* (King County, WA: King County Metro, October 2019), https://kingcounty.gov/~/media/depts/metro/about/planning/mobility-framework/metro-mobility-framework-report.pdf.

31. AAA Exchange, "Senior Driver Safety and Mobility," accessed March 1, 2023, https://exchange.aaa.com/safety/senior-driver-safety-mobility.

32. AARP, *Testimony of Shannon Guzman, MCP, on Behalf of AARP Before the Senate Committee on Banking, Housing and Urban Affairs on "Affordability and Accessibility: Addressing the*

Housing Needs of America's Seniors" (Washington, DC, March 31, 2022), 7, https://www.aarp.org/content/dam/aarp/poli tics/advocacy/2022/03/sen-banking-hearing-testimony-3-31 -22.pdf.

33. AARP, "Livable Communities Are Age Friendly," accessed March 1, 2023, https://www.aarp.org/livable-communities /about/.

34. Richard Read, "Nearly 20 Percent of U.S. Drivers Are over 65: Are America's Roads Ready for Them?" *Washington Post,* November 7, 2016, https://www.washingtonpost.com/cars /nearly-20-percent-of-us-drivers-are-over-65-are-americas -roads-ready-for-them/2016/11/07/1b70f292-a51b -11e6-ba46-53db57f0e351_story.html.

35. Abha Bhattarai, "Fewer Hot Showers, Less Meat: How Retirees on Fixed Incomes Are Dealing with Inflation," *Washington Post,* March 21, 2022, https://www.washingtonpost.com/busi ness/2022/03/21/elderly-inflation-fixed-income/.

36. Disability Mobility Initiative, "#WeekWithoutDriving 2022," March 8, 2023, YouTube video, https://www.youtube.com /watch?v=mSIBmv3a-WY.

37. WSLJTC, *Nondrivers.*

38. US Census Bureau, "American Community Survey," March 16, 2023, https://www.census.gov/programs-surveys/acs.

39. New York City Schools, "Transportation Eligibility," modified in 2019, https://www.schools.nyc.gov/school-life/trans portation/bus-eligibility.

40. Bureau of Transportation Statistics, "The Longer Route to School," January 12, 2021, https://www.bts.gov/topics/pas senger-travel/back-school-2019.

41. National Center for Education Statistics, "Students Transported

at Public Expense and Current Expenditures for Transportation," modified in 2019, https://nces.ed.gov/programs /digest/d19/tables/dt19_236.90.asp.

42. Monica Velez, "The Bus Rides to Seattle Schools Improved, but at What Cost?" *Seattle Times*, January 3, 2023, https:// www.seattletimes.com/education-lab/seattle-school-bus-service-improved-but-at-what-cost/.

43. Melissa Santos, "Seattle Schools Change Start Times to Save Money on Busing," *Axios*, August 30, 2023, https://www .axios.com/local/seattle/2023/08/30/seattle-schools-bus -schedule.

44. John Ransom, "Philadelphia School District Offers $300 a Month to Parents to Drive Their Kids to School," *Lion*, August 25, 2023, https://readlion.com/philadelphia-school-dist rict-offers-300-a-month-to-parents-to-drive-their-kids-to -school/.

45. Federal Highway Administration, US Department of Transportation, *Children's Travel to School: 2017 National Household Travel Survey* (Washington, DC: Federal Highway Administration, March 2019), https://nhts.ornl.gov/assets/FHWA _NHTS_%20Brief_Traveltoschool_032519.pdf.

46. Shannon Osaka, "'I'll Call an Uber or 911': Why Gen Z Doesn't Want to Drive," *Washington Post*, February 13, 2023, https://www.washingtonpost.com/climate-solutions/2023 /02/13/gen-z-driving-less-uber/.

47. Caitlin Gibson, "Why Teenagers Aren't Driving Anymore," *Washington Post*, February 21, 2023, https://www.washington post.com/parenting/2023/02/21/teens-not-driving/.

48. Kelcie Ralph and Evan Iacobucci, "Travel Mode and Participation in Structured Activities among U.S. Teens,"

Travel Behaviour and Society 25 (October 2021), https://doi.org/10.1016/j.tbs.2021.07.004.

49. City of SeaTac, "Basic Population Demographics," November 2017, https://www.seatacwa.gov/Home/ShowDocument?id=14865.

Chapter 2. What Nondrivers Need

1. Puget Sound Regional Council, "Coordinated Mobility Plan," May 26, 2022, https://www.psrc.org/planning-2050/regional-transportation-plan/coordinated-mobility-plan.

2. Bureau of Transportation Statistics, "Travel Patterns of American Adults with Disabilities," September 2018, https://www.bts.gov/travel-patterns-with-disabilities.

3. City of Seattle, "Seattle Sidewalk Accessibility Guide," accessed March 1, 2023, https://www.seattle.gov/transportation/projects-and-programs/programs/pedestrian-program/sidewalk-accessibility-guide.

4. Rooted in Rights, Disability Rights Washington, "Seattle's Snow Planning Freezes Out People with Disabilities," August 5, 2019, https://rootedinrights.org/video/snow/.

5. Yochai Eisenberg, Amy Heider, Robert G. Gould, and Robin L. Jones, "Are Communities in the United States Planning for Pedestrians with Disabilities? Findings from a Systematic Evaluation of Local Government Barrier Removal Plans," *Cities* 102 (July 2020), https://doi.org/10.1016/j.citics.2020.102720l.

6. Lonberg v. City of Riverside, 571 F.3d 846 (9th Cir. 2009).

7. Department of Justice, "ADA Best Practices Toolkit for State and Local Governments," May 7, 2007, https://archive.ada.gov/pcatoolkit/toolkitmain.htm.

8. James Elliott and Jeremy Chrzan, "PROWAG Adoption Marks Disability Rights Milestone," Toole Design, August 8, 2023, https://Tooledesign.Com/Insights/2023/08/Prowag-Adoption-Marks-Disability-Rights-Milestone/.

9. Governor's Highway Safety Association, "Pedestrian Deaths Hit 41-Year High in 2022 with More than 7,500 Killed," June 22, 2023, https://www.ghsa.org/about/news/Smart-Cities-Dive/Pedestrian-Deaths-Hit-41-Year-High23.

10. Hatem Abou-Senna, Essam Radwan, and Ayman Saber Mohamed, "Investigating the Correlation between Sidewalks and Pedestrian Safety," *Accident Analysis and Prevention* 166 (March 2022), https://doi.org/10.1016/j.aap.2021.106548.

11. Disability Mobility Initiative, "Greg—Longview," August 3, 2023, YouTube video, https://youtu.be/SSSV7I-FDBc.

12. Heather Meares, "How Do Roundabouts Affect Pedestrians Who Might Not See, Hear?" *Walla Walla Union Bulletin*, November 29, 2021, https://www.union-bulletin.com/opinion/opinion_columns/column-how-do-roundabouts-affect-pedestrians-who-might-not-see-hear/article_c1d787fa-4cdb-11ec-a8fb-f78b16776a23.html.

13. Disability Rights Advocates, "Federal Court Orders New York City to Install Thousands of Accessible Crosswalk Signals over the Next 10 Years," January 4, 2022, https://dralegal.org/featured/federal-court-orders-new-york-city-to-install-thousands-of-accessible-crosswalk-signals-over-the-next-10-years/.

14. Disability Rights Advocates, "Court Rules that Chicago's Intersections Must Be Made Accessible for Blind Pedestrians," April 6, 2023, https://dralegal.org/press/chicago-pedestrian-signals-ruling/.

15. Rooted In Rights, Disability Rights Washington, "Why Does

Signal Timing Matter? Carol Explains," September 27, 2019, https://rootedinrights.org/video/trafficsignals/.

16. Jessie Singer, *There Are No Accidents: The Deadly Rise of Injury and Disaster—Who Profits and Who Pays the Price* (New York: Simon and Schuster, 2023).

17. Todd Litman, "Transportation Cost and Benefit Analysis," Victoria Transport Policy Institute, October 2016, www.vtpi .org/tca.

18. Federal Highway Administration, US Department of Transportation, "Frequently Asked Questions—Part 4 Highway Traffic Signals—FHWA MUTCD," modified September 14, 2022, https://mutcd.fhwa.dot.gov/knowledge/faqs/faq_part4 .htm.

19. Disability Mobility Initiative, Disability Rights Washington, "Transportation Access for Everyone Storymap," https://www .disabilityrightswa.org/storymap/.

20. Transportation Research Board. "Building a Path to Better Active Transport: Understanding the Effects of Traffic Noise, Air Quality, and Vulnerable Road User Comfort on Users," Workshop 5008, January 2024. https://annualmeeting.mytrb .org/OnlineProgram/Details/20750.

21. Washington State Legislature Joint Transportation Committee (WSLJTC), *Nondrivers: Population, Demographics, and Analysis* (N.p.: Toole Design, Cascadia Consulting Group, and Strategic Research Associates, 2023), https://leg.wa.gov /JTC/Documents/Studies/Nondrivers%202022/Nondrivers StudyFinalReportSummaryReport.pdf.

22. Conor McCormick-Cavanagh, "Remembering Gang of 19 Forty Years after Denver Protests Changed Accessibility," *Westword*, July 4, 2018, https://www.westword.com/news

/disability-protesters-gang-of-19-remembered-in-denver-104
96346.

23. Federal Transit Administration, US Department of Transportation, "Enhanced Mobility of Seniors and Individuals with Disabilities—Section 5310," modified March 2022, https://www.transit.dot.gov/funding/grants/enhanced-mobility-seniors-individuals-disabilities-section-5310.

24. Rayla Bellis, "More than One Million Households without a Car in Rural America Need Better Transit," Smart Growth America, May 15, 2020, https://smartgrowthamerica.org/more-than-one-million-households-without-a-car-in-rural-america-need-better-transit/.

25. Sonam Vashi, "Greyhound Connects America—What Happens If Intercity Buses Disappear?" *National Geographic*, May 4, 2021, https://www.nationalgeographic.com/travel/article/photos-show-the-possibility-of-traveling-the-country-by-bus.

26. Danny Westneat, "The Story of the $1,200 Cab Ride Straight Out of Idaho," *Seattle Times*, September 9, 2022, https://www.seattletimes.com/seattle-news/the-story-of-the-1200-cab-ride-straight-out-of-idaho.

27. Jessica McDiarmid, *Highway of Tears: A True Story of Racism, Indifference, and the Pursuit of Justice for Missing and Murdered Indigenous Women and Girls* (New York: Simon and Schuster, 2019).

28. Rooted In Rights, Disability Rights Washington, "Disabled People Ride Bikes (and Trikes, and Tandems and Recumbents)!" March 1, 2021, https://www.youtube.com/watch?v=OzCPvsPGhbU.

29. In the summer of 2019, Peters collaborated with the BC Bike Coalition to bring mobility justice advocates from across the

US and Canada to speak at the Bike Coalition's annual conference. Being invited to participate in this conference, where Peters brought disabled advocates and people working in public
health together with seniors and immigrant and First Nation
communities, helped me start to imagine the possibility of
connecting disability mobility advocacy to other conversations about equity in public space.

30. Gabrielle Peters, "Accessibility Is Not a Competitive Sport," G
Peters (MsSineNomine) Substack, August 17, 2023, https://
mssinenomine.substack.com/p/accessibility-is-not-a-com
petitive?utm_campaign=post&utm_medium=web.

31. Bureau of Transportation Statistics, "Travel Patterns."

32. WSLJTC, *Nondrivers.*

33. US Bureau of Labor Statistics, "Persons with a Disability: Labor Force Characteristics—2022," February 23, 2023, https://
www.bls.gov/news.release/pdf/disabl.pdf.

34. Center for American Progress, "Advancing Economic Security for People With Disabilities," July 26, 2019, https://www
.americanprogress.org/article/advancing-economic-security
-people-disabilities/.

35. Easterseals Project Action, "The Americans with Disabilities
Act and You: Frequently Asked Questions on Taxicab Service," August 2007, https://www.nadtc.org/wp-content/up
loads/NADTC-Taxicab-ADA-Brochure-PDF-version.pdf.

36. Jose Martinez and Suhail Bhat, "TLC Blows by Deadline in
Struggle to Get 50% of City Taxis Wheelchair Accessible,"
The City, March 16, 2022, https://www.thecity.nyc/2022
/3/15/22979913/tlc-blows-by-deadline-in-struggle-to-get-50
-of-city-taxis-wheelchair-accessible.

37. Eno Center for Transportation, "Taxing New Mobility Services,"

July 23, 2018, https://enotrans.org/eno-resources/eno-brief
-taxing-new-mobility-services-whats-right-whats-next/.

38. Becca Savransky, "King County Only Has 50 Wheelchair
Accessible Taxi Medallions—Advocates Have Wanted More
for Years," *Seattle PI*, October 2, 2019, https://www.seattlepi
.com/news/article/King-County-only-has-50-wheelchair-ac
cessible-14474515.php.

39. National Federation of the Blind, "Uber, Lyft, and Service Animals: The Discrimination Continues," April 13, 2020, https://
nfb.org/blog/uber-lyft-and-service-animals-discrimina
tion-continues.

40. Michelle Delgado, "U.S. House Prices Are Rising Exponen-
tially Faster than Income (2021 Data)," *Real Estate Witch*,
February 17, 2023, https://www.realestatewitch.com/house
-price-to-income-ratio-2021/.

41. WSLJTC, *Nondrivers.*

42. Bureau of Transportation Statistics, "Travel Patterns."

43. Bureau of Transportation Statistics, "Travel Patterns."

44. WSLJTC, *Nondrivers.*

45. Kelcie Ralph, "Childhood Car Access: Long-Term Consequences for Education, Emplaoyment, and Earnings," *Journal
of Planning Education and Research* 42, no. 1 (October 2018),
https://doi.org/10.1177/0739456x18798451.

46. Office of Disability Employment Policy, *Disability and the
Digital Divide: Internet Subscriptions, Internet Use and Employment Outcomes* (Washington, DC: United States Department
of Labor, 2022), https://www.dol.gov/sites/dolgov/files/OD
EP/pdf/disability-digital-divide-brief.pdf.

47. Mimi Sheller, *Mobility Justice: The Politics of Movement in an
Age of Extremes* (New York: Verso, 2018).

48. Eric Klinenberg, "Adaptation," *New Yorker*, December 31,

2012, https://www.newyorker.com/magazine/2013/01/07/adaptation-eric-klinenberg.

Chapter 3. Nondrivers Need What Everyone Needs

1. Wisconsin Department of Transportation, "Wisconsin Non-Driver Advisory Committee," accessed June 10, 2023, https://wisconsindot.gov/Pages/about-wisdot/who-we-are/comm-couns/windac.aspx.
2. Michelle Baruchman, "Are You Walking More During the Coronavirus Pandemic? Here's What People Are Noticing and What They Say Can Be Improved," *Seattle Times,* April 15, 2020, https://www.seattletimes.com/seattle-news/transportation/are-you-walking-more-during-the-coronavirus-pandemic-heres-what-people-are-noticing-and-what-they-say-can-be-improved/.
3. Anna Goodman, Anthony A. Laverty, Jamie Furlong, and Rachel Aldred, "The Impact of 2020 Low Traffic Neighbourhoods on Levels of Car/Van Driving among Residents: Findings from Lambeth, London, UK," *Findings* (June 2023), https://doi.org/10.32866/001c.75470.
4. Taskar Center for Accessible Technology, University of Washington, "OpenSidewalks," modified July 20, 2021, https://tcat.cs.washington.edu/2021/07/20/opensidewalks/.
5. University of Washington, "Transportation Data Equity Initiative," accessed June 10, 2023, https://transitequity.cs.washington.edu/.
6. Washington State Department of Transportation, "Active Transportation Plan," https://wsdot.wa.gov/construction-planning/statewide-plans/active-transportation-plan.
7. Washington State Department of Transportation, "Active Transportation Plan."

8. City of Oakland, "Sidewalk Certification FAQ," April 24, 2023, https://www.oaklandca.gov/resources/sidewalk-certification-faq.

9. Denver Deserves Sidewalks, "Vote Yes on 307," accessed June 10, 2023, https://denverdeservessidewalks.wordpress.com/.

10. John Greenfield, "Great News! Plow the Sidewalks Pilot Program Ordinance Passed City Council Today," *Streetsblog Chicago*, July 19, 2023, https://chi.streetsblog.org/2023/07/19/great-news-plow-the-sidewalks-pilot-program-ordinance-passed-in-city-council-today/.

11. City of Seattle, "New Sidewalks and Walkways," September 15, 2022, https://storymaps.arcgis.com/stories/dcbcd0bd0d4d4c4e9a580b8ff797da0b.

12. Janelle Retka, "Pedestrian Safety Is an Issue in the Lower Yakima Valley. The Yakama Nation Is Working on Plans for a New Trail System," *Yakima Herald-Republic*, February 21, 2020, https://www.yakimaherald.com/pedestrian-safety-is-an-issue-in-the-lower-yakima-valley-the-yakama-nation-is-working/article_c7a5de81-9ca6-5019-9c7e-67b01c038855.html.

13. Methow Trails, "Twisp to Winthrop Trail," accessed June 6, 2023, https://methowtrails.org/initiatives/twisp-to-winthrop-trail.

14. Max Harrison-Caldwell, "Champion of Disabled and Seniors Says Car-Free JFK Can Work for Everyone, with Provisions," *Medium*, April 26, 2022, https://thefrisc.com/champion-of-disabled-and-seniors-says-car-free-jfk-can-work-for-everyone-with-provisions-56006f20b03.

15. San Francisco Metropolitan Transportation Agency, *Guidelines for Accessible Building Blocks for Bicycle Facilities* (San Francisco: SFMTA, 2017), https://www.sfmta.com/sites/dc

fault/files/reports-and-documents/2017/11/2203-20140930
_buildingblocksfinal.pdf.

16. Natasha Opfell, *Getting to the Curb: A Guide to Building Protected Bike Lanes That Work for Pedestrians* (San Francisco: Walk San Francisco, 2019), https://walksf.org/wp-content/uploads/2019/12/getting-to-the-curb-report-final-walk-sf-2019.pdf.

17. Laura Bliss, "Should SUVs Get a Pedestrian Warning Label?" *Bloomberg Citylab*, May 24, 2021, https://www.bloomberg.com/news/articles/2021-05-24/pedestrian-safety-ratings-target-suvs-and-pickups/.

18. Federal Register, "Exemptions from Average Fuel Economy Standards; Passenger Automobile Average Fuel Economy Standards," July 1, 2022, https://www.federalregister.gov/documents/2022/07/01/2022-12618/exemptions-from-average-fuel-economy-standards-passenger-automobile-average-fuel-economy-standards.

19. Truck Safety Coalition, "Speed Limiters," September 3, 2021, https://trucksafety.org/speed-limiters/.

20. Diana Ionescu, "New York City to Test Speed Limiting Tech on City Vehicles," *Planetizen News*, August 23, 2022, https://www.planetizen.com/news/2022/08/118405-new-york-city-test-speed-limiting-tech-city-vehicles.

21. National Highway Traffic Safety Administration, "NHTSA Proposes Automatic Emergency Braking Requirements for New Vehicles," May 31, 2023, https://www.nhtsa.gov/press-releases/automatic-emergency-braking-proposed-rule.

22. Nicholas Bloom, *The Great American Transit Disaster: A Century of Austerity, Auto-Centric Planning, and White Flight* (Chicago: University of Chicago Press, 2023).

23. US Department of Transportation, "Biden-Harris Admini-

stration Announces $686 Million in Grants to Modernize Older Transit Stations and Improve Accessibility across the Country," December 19, 2022, https://www.transportation .gov/briefing-room/biden-harris-administration-announces -686-million-grants-modernize-older-transit.

24. Kevin Duggan, "SMILE! Bus Lane Cameras Reduce Colli sions, Speed Commutes, MTA Says," *Streetsblog New York City,* June 12, 2023, https://nyc.streetsblog.org/2023/04/25 /smile-bus-lane-cameras-reduce-collisions-speed-up-com mutes-according-to-mta-stats.

25. Washington State Legislature Joint Transportation Commit- tee (WSLJTC), *Nondrivers: Population, Demographics, and Analysis* (N.p.: Toole Design, Cascadia Consulting Group, and Strategic Research Associates, 2023), https://leg.wa.gov /JTC/Documents/Studies/Nondrivers%202022/Nondrivers StudyFinalReportSummaryReport.pdf.

26. King County Metro, "Metro's Subsidized Annual Pass Fea- tured in National Case Study," September 24, 2021, https:// kingcountymetro.blog/2021/09/16/metros-subsidized-annu al-pass-featured-in-national-case-study/.

27. TransitCenter, "Transit's Looming Fiscal Cliff: How Bad Is It and What Can We Do?" April 7, 2023, https://transitcen ter.org/transits-fiscal-cliff-why-we-need-a-new-funding-para digm/.

28. Front and Centered and Center for Neighborhood Technol- ogy, "Washington Transit Access Map," November 2022, https://watransitaccessmap.org/.

29. Washington State Department of Transportation, *Frequent Transit Service Study Final Report* (Olympia: Washington State Department of Transportation, June 2023), https://

wsdot.wa.gov/sites/default/files/2023-06/Frequent-Transit-Service
-Study-Final-Report-June2023.pdf.

30. Urban Institute, "The Ways Transit Agencies Adapted during the Pandemic Can Inform an Equitable Recovery," November 30, 2021, https://www.urban.org/urban-wire/ways-transit -agencies-adapted-during-pandemic-can-inform-equitable-re covery.

31. TransitCenter, "Bus Operators in Crisis," October 25, 2022, https://transitcenter.org/publication/bus-operators-in-crisis/.

32. Martin Kidston, "Montana 'Closer than Ever' in Restoration of Southern Rail Passenger Route," KPAX News, March 6, 2023, https://www.kpax.com/news/montana-news/montana -closer-than-ever-in-restoration-of-southern-rail-passenger -route.

33. Transit Wiki, "Tripper Rule," accessed July 6, 2023, https:// transitwiki.org/TransitWiki/index.php/Tripper_Rule.

34. Pacific Northwest Transportation Research Consortium, Region 10, "Incorporating Ride-Sourcing Service into ADA Paratransit," December 6, 2021, https://depts.washington .edu/pactrans/incorporating-ride-sourcing-service-into-ada -paratransit/.

35. Rachel Urgana, "Los Angeles Public Rideshare Is Popular and Expensive," *Governing*, September 14, 2023, https://www .governing.com/transportation/los-angeles-public-rideshare -is-popular-and-expensive.

36. Jeff McMurray, "What If Public Transit Was Like Uber? A Small City Ended Its Bus Service to Find Out," ABC News, September 15, 2023, https://abcnews.go.com/US/wire Story/public-transit-uber-small-city-ended-bus-service-103 244215.

37. Mi Diao, Hui Kong, and Jinhua Zhao, "Impacts of Transportation Network Companies on Urban Mobility," *Nature Sustainability* 4, no. 6 (2021): 494–500, https://doi.org/10.1038/s41893-020-00678-z.

38. Paris Marx, *Road to Nowhere: What Silicon Valley Gets Wrong about the Future of Transportation* (New York: Verso, 2022).

39. Disability Rights Education Defense Fund, "Addressing Disability and Ableist Bias in Autonomous Vehicles: Ensuring Safety, Equity and Accessibility in Detection, Collision Algorithms and Data Collection," November 7, 2022, https://dredf.org/2023/03/09/addressing-disability-and-ableist-bias-in-autonomous-vehicles-ensuring-safety-equity-and-accessibility-in-detection-collision-algorithms-and-data-collection/.

40. Alex Keating, "Opinion: Bloomington, Ind. Makes Smart Move to Mandate Seated Vehicles in Its Micromobility Program," *Streetsblog USA,* May 31, 2023, https://usa.streetsblog.org/2023/04/28/opinion-bloomington-ind-makes-smart-move-to-mandate-seated-vehicles-in-its-micromobility-program.

41. Veo Micromobility, "Bronx," June 9, 2022, https://www.veoride.com/bronx/.

42. Laura Bliss, "The Power of Electric Bike Libraries," *Bloomberg Citylab*, October 15, 2021, https://www.bloomberg.com/news/articles/2021-10-15/e-bike-lending-libraries-aim-to-boost-adoption.

43. Sam Brasch, "Colorado Charges Ahead with E-Bike Rebates for Low- and Moderate-Income Residents," Colorado Public Radio, June 8, 2023, https://www.cpr.org/2023/06/08/colorado-ebike-rebate-program/.

44. David Zipper, "Golf Carts—Golf Carts!—Are the Transportation of the Future," *Slate Magazine,* August 15, 2022,

https://slate.com/business/2022/08/golf-carts-transportation-future-peachtree-city.html.

45. Ari Ne'eman and Nicole Maestas, "How Has COVID-19 Impacted Disability Employment?" *Disability and Health Journal* 16, no. 2 (December 1, 2022): 101429, https://doi.org/10.1016/j.dhjo.2022.101429.

46. US Bureau of Labor Statistics, "Persons with a Disability: Labor Force Characteristics—2022," February 23, 2023, https://www.bls.gov/news.release/pdf/disabl.pdf.

47. Veterans Benefits and Health Care, "Health Services Research & Development," updated July 7, 2023, https://www.hsrd.research.va.gov/research_topics/access.cfm.

48. DispatchHealth, "Urgent Medical Care," accessed June 15, 2023, https://www.dispatchhealth.com/.

49. Malcolm Harris, *Palo Alto: A History of California, Capitalism, and the World* (New York: Hachette, 2023).

50. Kitty Krupat and Ligia M. Guallpa, "Los Deliveristas Unidos and the Ideals of Worker Justice," *New Labor Forum*, May 15, 2023, https://newlaborforum.cuny.edu/2023/05/10/los-deliveristas-unidos-and-the-ideals-of-worker-justice.

51. Mitchell Clark, "Seattle's New Law Gives Gig Workers Paid Sick Time Off," *Verge*, March 29, 2023, https://www.theverge.com/2023/3/29/23661878/seattle-gig-workers-paid-sick-time-uber-eats-doordash.

52. Seattle City Council Central Staff, "Comprehensive Plan Proposals for 2022–2023," July 27, 2022, http://seattle.legistar.com/View.ashx?M=F&ID=11085456&GUID=95FE6D78-425A-4367-A529-4C0C2E922DC6.

53. Jonathan Maus, "It's Now a Portland City Code Violation to Deny 'Drive-Thru' Service to Bicycle Users," *Bike Portland*, May 30, 2018, https://bikeportland.org/2018/05/29/its-now

-against-portland-city-code-to-deny-drive-thru-service-to-bi
cycle-users-282407.

54. Nathaniel Meyersohn, "Why Cities Want to Ban New Drive-Thrus," CNN, June 24, 2023, https://www.cnn.com/2023/06/24/business/drive-thru-fast-food-chick-fil-a-urban-planning/index.html.

55. Heidi Groover, "How to Get Tested for Coronavirus in Seattle If You Don't Have a Car," *Seattle Times*, April 9, 2020, https://www.seattletimes.com/seattle-news/transportation/coronavirus-drive-thru-testing-brings-extra-challenges-for-people-who-dont-drive.

56. Tom Fucoloro, "Under New Law, Washington Communities Must Plan around 'Multimodal Level of Service,'" *Seattle Bike Blog*, May 3, 2023, https://www.seattlebikeblog.com/2023/05/03/under-new-law-washington-communities-must-plan-around-multimodal-level-of-service/.

Chapter 4. Valuing the Expertise of Nondrivers

1. City of Seattle, *2020 Greenhouse Gas Inventory* (Seattle: Seattle Office of Sustainability and Environment, October 2022), https://www.seattle.gov/documents/Departments/OSE/ClimateDocs/GHG%20Inventory/2020_GHG_Inventory_Oct_2022.pdf.

2. Front and Centered, *Just Movement Listening Sessions and Survey Findings* (Seattle: Front and Centered, 2021), https://frontandcentered.org/wp-content/uploads/2021/02/FC-Transportation-Listening-Session-Report.pdf.

3. National Center for Mobility Management, *Higher Education Practices to Prepare Future Transportation Professionals Regarding Disability, Accessibility, and Mobility Management* (Washington, DC: National Center for Mobility Management,

2022), https://nationalcenterformobilitymanagement.org/wp -content/uploads/2022/06/Career-Brief-Final4.pdf.

4. Easterseals, "Easterseals and NADTC Online Learning Portal: Course Categories," accessed June 6, 2023, https://learn.eas terseals.com/course/index.php.

5. AARP, "Walk Audit Tool Kit," 2022, www.aarp.org/walk audit.

6. National Association of Chronic Disease Directors, "Walk-ability Action Institute," accessed June 6, 2023, https://chro nicdisease.org/page/wai/.

7. Jonathon Stalls, *Walk: Slow Down, Wake Up, and Connect at 1–3 Miles per Hour* (New York: Penguin Random House, 2023).

8. Caitlin Rogger, "WMATA's Transfer Penalty Finally Gets the Boot," *Greater Greater Washington,* June 21, 2021, https://ggw ash.org/view/81706/wmatas-transfer-penalty-finally-gets-the -boot.

9. Disability Rights Washington, "Week Without Driving 2022 Announced with Proclamation from Governor Inslee," August 1, 2022, https://www.disabilityrightswa.org/week-without -driving-2022-announced-with-proclamation-from-governor-in slee-and-video-invite-from-washington-elected-leaders.

10. Disability Mobility Initiative, "Week Without Driving 2022."

11. Disability Mobility Initiative, "King County Councilmember Claudia Balducci on #WeekWithoutDriving," September 16, 2022, https://www.youtube.com/watch?v=fs8o2hMwZT8.

12. Disability Mobility Initiative, "Week Without Driving 2022."

13. Disability Mobility Initiative, "Week Without Driving 2022."

14. Disability Mobility Initiative, "Week Without Driving—2023 Promo," YouTube video, July 9, 2023, https://www.youtube .com/watch?v=BsX8iok_cyc.

15. Mike Lindblom, "This WA 'Boulevard of Death' Is Used by 30,000 Drivers a Day," *Seattle Times*, July 1, 2023, https://www.seattletimes.com/seattle-news/transportation/just-out side-seattle-residents-endure-a-dangerous-yet-ordinary -crossroads/.

16. Introducing Youth to American Infrastructure, accessed June 10, 2023, https://iyai.org/.

17. King County Metro, "Mobility Framework," May 1, 2019, https://kingcounty.gov/depts/transportation/metro/about /policies/mobility-framework.aspx.

18. TransitCenter, *Who Rules Transit? An Analysis of Who Holds Power in Transit Agency Decision Making and How It Should Change* (New York: TransitCenter, 2022), https://transitcen ter.org/publication/who-rules-transit-2/.

19. Intercity Transit, "Who Governs Intercity Transit?" accessed June 28, 2023, https://www.intercitytransit.com/about-us /transit-authority.

20. Transportation Choices Coalition, "Transit Talk: How Riders Can Shape Transportation," June 21, 2023, https://transpor tationchoices.org/join-our-next-webinar-transit-talk-how -riders-can-shape-transportation/.

21. Bureau of Transportation Statistics, "Travel Patterns of American Adults with Disabilities," September 2018, https://www .bts.gov/travel-patterns-with-disabilities.

22. National Center for Mobility Management, *Higher Education Practices.*

23. Sonia Sarkar, "Disability Justice—in the Workplace (and Beyond)," *Nonprofit Quarterly*, March 2, 2023, https://non profitquarterly.org/disability-justice-in-the-workplace-and -beyond/.

Conclusion

1. Peter Norton, *Fighting Traffic: The Dawn of the Motor Age in the American City* (Cambridge, MA: MIT Press, 2008); Peter Norton, *Autonorama: The Illusory Promise of High-Tech Driving* (Washington, DC: Island Press, 2021).

2. Nicholas Bloom, *The Great American Transit Disaster: A Century of Austerity, Auto-Centric Planning, and White Flight* (Chicago: University of Chicago Press, 2023).

About the Author

Anna Zivarts is a low-vision mom and nondriver who was born with the neurological condition nystagmus. Since launching the Disability Mobility Initiative at Disability Rights Washington in 2020, Zivarts has worked to bring the voices of nondrivers to the planning and policy-making tables through organizing, research, and policy campaigns led by nondrivers. Zivarts serves on the Pacific Northwest Transportation Consortium advisory board and the National Aging and Disability Transportation Center's Coordination Advisory Committee. She began her career as an organizer and videographer, producing videos and collecting stories for the LGBT & HIV/AIDS and Voting Rights projects at the American Civil Liberties Union, and cofounding the union and worker-run video production company Time of Day Media. Zivarts earned her undergraduate and master's degrees from Stanford University.